PENGUIN VEER
1965: COURAGE UNLEASHED

Major General Ian Cardozo was commissioned at the Indian Military Academy into the 1st Battalion the 5th Gorkha Rifles (Frontier Force), where he received his basic grounding as a young officer. Thereafter, he took part in the Sino–Indian war of 1962, the Indo–Pak war of 1965 and the Indo–Pak war of 1971. He fought the 1965 and 1971 wars with the 4th Battalion the 5th Gorkha Rifles (FF).

Wounded in the battle of Sylhet in Bangladesh, he overcame the disability of losing a leg and became the first war-disabled officer of the Indian Army to be approved for command of an infantry battalion and brigade. He thereafter commanded an infantry division and retired as chief of staff of a corps in the North-east. On retirement, he worked in the area of disability with an NGO and as vice president of the War Wounded Foundation, before being appointed by the Government of India as chairman of the Rehabilitation Council of India, where he worked for nine years.

He is a military historian, war poet and author of *1971: Stories of Grit and Glory from the Indo–Pak War* and *Beyond Fear: True Stories on Life in the Indian Armed Forces*, among other titles. His books, poems and autobiography, *Cartoos Saab: A Soldier's Story of Resilience in Adversity,* have been widely acclaimed. His poems on war have been set to music and feature worldwide on leading music platforms. He is also working with an illustrator on graphic novels about the courage and competence of the Indian soldier, of which fifteen have been published so far.

1965

COURAGE UNLEASHED

SHORT STORIES ON THE INDO-PAK WAR

IAN CARDOZO

PENGUIN
VEER

An imprint of Penguin Random House

PENGUIN VEER

Penguin Veer is an imprint of the Penguin Random House group of companies whose addresses can be found at global.penguinrandomhouse.com

Published by Penguin Random House India Pvt. Ltd
4th Floor, Capital Tower 1, MG Road,
Gurugram 122 002, Haryana, India

Penguin
Random House
India

First published in Penguin Veer by Penguin Random House India 2024

Copyright © Ian Cardozo 2024

Sketches courtesy of the author, except on pages 136, 149, 156, 165 and 192—sketches courtesy of Dr Arun Cardozo

All rights reserved

10 9 8 7 6 5 4 3 2 1

The views and opinions expressed in this book are the author's own and the facts are as reported by him which have been verified to the extent possible, and the publishers are not in any way liable for the same.

Please note that no part of this book may be used or reproduced in any manner for the purpose of training artificial intelligence technologies or systems.

ISBN 9780143460374

Typeset in Requiem Text by MAP Systems, Bengaluru, India
Printed at Thomson Press India Ltd, New Delhi

This book is sold subject to the condition that it shall not, by way of trade or otherwise, be lent, resold, hired out, or otherwise circulated without the publisher's prior consent in any form of binding or cover other than that in which it is published and without a similar condition including this condition being imposed on the subsequent purchaser.

www.penguin.co.in

MIX
Paper | Supporting
responsible forestry
FSC® C010615

*To those who died defending India
during the Indo—Pak war of 1965
and those who kept the home fires burning
while their men were away*

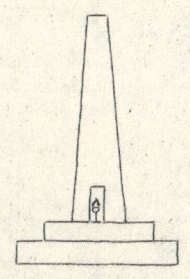

The National War Memorial

Contents

Acknowledgements ix
Preface xvii
Synopsis xxi

1. Combat above Kharagpur — 1
2. At the Gates of Lahore — 18
3. Valour Personified — 46
4. Asal Uttar — 55
5. Chhamb Battleground — 74
6. The Avengers — 99
7. A Mission Fulfilled — 113
8. Ambushed! — 121
9. Jumbahadur — 140
10. Twists of Fate — 155
11. Badmash — 184
12. The 1965 War—Success or Failure? — 212

Afterword 215
Glossary 221
Notes 225
Bibliography 233

Acknowledgements

'War comes at a time when the country can least afford it.'

—Anonymous

The persons I wish to thank first are the protagonists in these stories. As active participants in battle, it is they who have made these stories come alive. There are others who are part of these stories or who have contributed in some way orally or in writing to prove that real life is often stranger than fiction.

Their names are appended below in no particular order:

Brigadier Desmond Hayde, MVC
Squadron Leader Alfred Cooke, VrC
General Arun Vaidya, PVSM, MVC*, AVSM
Squadron Leader Rana Chhina, MBE
Colonel Madan Bhatia
Shiv Kunal Verma
Major General A.J.S. Sandhu, VSM
Air Marshal Bharat Kumar, PVSM, AVSM
Lieutenant General Satish Talwar, PVSM, AVSM, VSM

Colonel Sunith Cardozo
Santosh Kumar Pal
Manish Bawa
Nitika Verma
Krit Verma
Air Marshal Phillip Rajkumar, PVSM, AVSM
Dr Arun Cardozo
Vikram Cardozo
Shilpa Vijayan
JC-11111 Subedar Bhimbahadur Rana
Naib Subedar Narbahadur Gurung
Naik Dilijang Gurung
Naik Damarbahadur Gurung
Havildar Karnabahadur Gurung
Naik Kharkabahadur Gurung
Naib Subedar Prem Singh
Major General Balwant Singh Ahluwalia
Wing Commander Om Taneja, VrC
Brigadier T.K. Theogaraj, MVC
Brigadier J.B.F. Fridell
Major General Salim Caleb, MVC
Major General Farhat Bhatty, VSM, MiD
Major General Jogindar Singh, VSM
CQMH Abdul Hamid, PVC
P.V.S. Jagan Mohan
Samir Chopra
Squadron Leader A.B. (Tubby) Devayya, MVC
Air Marshal Denzil Keelor, PVSM, AVSM, VrC
1st Battalion the 5th Gorkha Rifles (FF)
4th Battalion the 5th Gorkha Rifles (FF)
4 Grenadiers
3 Jat

3 Cav
Deccan Horse

In addition to the names given above, I would also like to acknowledge those who have made a special contribution to these stories. They are:

Brigadier Desmond Hayde, MVC, for his narration of the story of the battle of Dograi and the major part he played in taking his battalion to the gates of Lahore. His outstanding leadership is an example to the present and future generations of officers and soldiers of the Indian Army. This story is mostly in his own words and much of this account has been gleaned from his personal narration in a pamphlet titled 'The Battle of Dograi', issued by the United Service Institution of India and from my personal interaction with the Brigadier in correspondence, and in long discussions on war in general and in this battle in particular.

CQMH Abdul Hamid, PVC, whose outstanding leadership in the story 'Valour Personified' motivated his team to take on the might of Pakistan's 1st Armoured Division. His personal score of three Patton tanks with his RCL gun won for him the Param Vir Chakra. His destruction of four more Patton tanks on subsequent days of the battle has made his memory eternal and part of the folklore of the Indian Army.

The officers and the jawans of the Indian Army and the kisans of Punjab, for their raw courage at the battle of Asal Uttar that helped destroy more than half of the Patton tanks of Pakistan's 1st Armoured Division. The story 'Asal Uttar' underlines the meaning of the name of this village that was the 'True Answer' to Pakistan's offensive operation towards Amritsar and the Beas River. Despite one of the biggest tank battles after World War II raging all around them, the farmers of Punjab continued to tend to their crops and when it was no longer possible to work their fields, they flooded them with water, which proved to be a nemesis for Pakistani tanks. The tanks got bogged down in the fields and became target practice for Indian tank gunners, giving rise to the slogan *'Jai Jawan! Jai Kisan!'*

Squadron Leader Alfred Cooke, VrC, of the Indian Air Force who took on four Pakistani F-86 Sabre jets, destroying one, badly damaging another and getting behind a third, only to find that he had run out of ammunition. The account of his story 'Combat above Kharagpur' makes for exciting reading. The professors and students of IIT Kharagpur are the only ones who witnessed this epic air battle on the morning of 7 September 1965, as the Indian and Pakistani pilots battled it out to take control of the sky. I was fortunate to be able to look at Alfred Cooke's detailed interview when he visited the United Service Institution of India, which has helped me in the writing of this story.

JC-1111 Subedar Bhimbahadur Rana, also known as 'Ek Saab' (because of the number of ones in his personal number), my second-in-command of Alpha Company, 4th Battalion the 5th Gorkha Rifles (FF), during the 1965 war—an outstanding JCO—who always wanted to be the first to tackle the enemy and did so when we were ambushed by an overwhelming number of guerrillas of Nusrat Force of Pakistan's Operation Gibraltar and who chopped off the head of the Pakistani Rocket Launcher No. 1 and was killed while decapitating another. Unfortunately, his bravery has not been recognized.

Acknowledgements

Wing Commander 'Omi Taneja', VrC, who was responsible for dispatching the second raid on Sargodha, setting a benchmark for leadership and competence in battle, by making sure he did what was right, irrespective of the consequences. It was a big risk, but he took it and he proved to be right. The account of the first raid, which is a gripping story, is narrated in 'It's Never Too Late' in my earlier book, *Beyond Fear*.

Major General Jogindar Singh, VSM (1st Class), whose critical analysis of the planning and conduct of the 1965 war as Chief of Staff Western Command in his book *Behind the Scene* needs to be looked at. Of special significance is what happened at Chhamb before, during and after the battle.

Air Marshal Denzil Keelor, PVSM, AVSM, VrC, for his narration of the account of how the Gnats took on the Sabres after the destruction of the Vampires over Chhamb and earning for the Gnats the sobriquet Sabre Slayers.

Shiv Kunal Verma, whose book *1965: A Western Sunrise—India's War with Pakistan,* helped considerably in filling in the details of the stories in this book. His ability to research and go into minor details is mind-boggling.

Major General A.J.S. Sandhu, VSM (Abdo), whose knowledge of the battles fought in Chhamb is acknowledged and well known on both sides of the border. His review of my story on the Chhamb battle helped me put together what happened at Chhamb in 1965.

P.V.S. Jagan Mohan and Samir Chopra, whose book *The Pakistan Air War of 1965* has been a major source of my stories of the air battles fought by the Indian Air Force during the 1965 Indo–Pak war.

Commanding Officer 4 Grenadiers, Maj. Gen. Farhat Bhatty, VSM, MiD, and the officers and jawans of 4 Grenadiers, who played an outstanding role in helping decimate Pakistan's 1st Armoured Division in the initial stage of the battle of Asal Uttar. 'Valour Personified' tells the story of how single individuals can contribute to victory in war.

Jumbahadur, my batman and runner during the battle of Gajna, who got killed by my side. This story is a tribute to Jumbahadur and the simple Gorkha soldier who braves danger and gives his all without counting the cost.

Manish Bawa, who has been a constant help in all my writings by assisting me to put my illustrations in the right configuration for my books and in particular, this book on the 1965 war. He and his tech-savvy assistants Nitika (ten years old) and Krit (eight years old) helped me sort out my laptop and saved my stories when it gave me a lot of trouble.

The stories of 'Badmash', 'Jumbahadur' and 'Ambushed!' are from my personal experiences of the 1965 war. Since these are my stories, I have no one in particular to thank except those who are part of the narratives, without whom it would not be possible for these stories to be told. I am grateful to all of them for being part of these stories and my life.

Lieutenant General Satish Talwar, PVSM, AVSM, VSM, my course mate, who was selected for the Staff College course at Queenscliff, Australia, because of his high order of merit in the selection process. His description of the course has helped me in narrating what happened there, as a prelude to what would happen subsequently in the 1971 war in the story of 'Twists of Fate'.

Brigadier N.B. Singh, whose description of what happened at Dera Baba Nanak (DBN) in the Indo–Pak war of 1965 finds place in the beginning of the story of '*Twists of Fate*'.

Santosh Pal, who has been a great help in sequencing the stories, designing this book and putting it together in its present form.

Meghna Girish, who has edited this book and all my books before they go to the publisher and whose ideas and suggestions have made this book what it is. This book is as much hers as it is mine.

Priscilla Cardozo, whose constant support has been my strength in all the years that we have been together and her generosity to let me write, although it keeps me away from her in the evening of our lives.

There are other wonderful persons who influenced my thoughts to shape these stories and without whom there would be no stories to tell. To all of them I offer my grateful thanks.

A soldier of the 5th Gorkha Rifles

Preface

'The evening of life is determined by the morning of it
The end is determined by the beginning
The decisions you make today, will play out tomorrow.'

—Anonymous

The stories in this book recount what happened during the Indo–Pak war of 1965. Although the official history of this war has been written, history is not everybody's cup of tea. In order to make the war and battles fought more easily understood by readers with no military background, I am presenting the history of this war in the form of short stories.

Many battles were fought during this war, but it has not been possible to narrate all of them. I have had to choose between what was desirable and what was possible, within the limits of space.

These are stories of 'courage beyond fear and duty above death' that highlight the values of love for one's country and its people, of honour from which all values emanate, the concept that no sacrifice is too great for the nation, of willpower, of the spirit of never giving up, and the determination to win because victory is what war is all about.

The stories in this book are about the Indian Army and the Indian Air Force. The Government of India did not permit the Indian Navy to undertake offensive operations in this war. At that time, in the perspective of the government, the priority of the Navy lay in the Bay of Bengal, where Indonesia had ambitions to capture and take over some of the Nicobar Islands and the Government did not want to extend the war to the western seaboard. The remarkable way in which the Indian Navy took to the offensive in 1971 to make up for what it was denied in 1965, is a story by itself, which finds place in the synopsis of the story of this war.

The Indian citizen needs to know more about how the military functions in war and peace, because they too have a stake in the security and well-being of the nation, and their opinions matter. The written style of this work is reader-friendly and shorn, as far as possible, of military baggage, so as to make the stories easy to understand. Some of the stories are from my personal experience but most are the exploits of others.

Reading the synopsis, before reading the stories, would make one understand the narratives better. The bibliography at the end of the book lists reading material on the 1965 war for those who want to know more about that war, and the glossary gives military terminology that could not be avoided.

Writing about these wonderful stories does not mean that we did not make mistakes. We could have done better, but one needs to recognize that those decisions were made under circumstances that were not of one's choosing. However, it is up to persons at the head of affairs in the armed forces to learn from those mistakes and ensure that they are not repeated.

I hope these stories will bring the armed forces closer to the citizens of our country, particularly those young men and women who are looking for adventure in uniform.

Ian Cardozo
April 2024

Synopsis

'If Pakistan has any ideas of annexing any part of our territories by force, she should think afresh. I want to state categorically, that force will be met with force and aggression against us will never be allowed to succeed.'

—former Prime Minister Lal Bahadur Shastri[1]

Pakistan's obsession to take the state of Jammu and Kashmir (J & K) by force tempted it once again in 1965 to replicate an earlier attempt of 1947–48. India had suffered a severe reverse in the Sino-Indian War of 1962, her economy had suffered substantially and reorganization of her forces was incomplete. Pandit Nehru had passed away and President Ayub Khan and his Pakistani generals who ruled Pakistan did not think that the diminutive Lal Bahadur Shastri was a leader they would have trouble contending with. They felt that all the advantages to strike at the state of J & K were in their favour, and it was unlikely that such an opportunity would ever occur again. The military received the support of Pakistan's foreign minister, Zulfikar Ali Bhutto.

Pakistan had earlier entered into a military pact with the United States of America (US) and soon after, joined the Central Treaty Organization (CENTO) and the Southeast Asia Treaty Organization (SEATO). In return, Pakistan received 1.5 billion dollars in economic assistance and massive military aid from the US. The military equipment included 400 M-48 Patton tanks, two squadrons of M-24 Chaffee tanks, one squadron of F-104A supersonic Starfighter jets, four squadrons of F-86 Sabre jets, two squadrons of B-57 bombers, artillery guns to equip heavy and medium artillery regiments and substantial communication equipment. Pakistan had also obtained lasting support from China by illegally ceding the Shaksgam Valley to China—land that was disputed with India and was not Pakistan's to give away. In return, China assured Pakistan of support in the form of military equipment and assistance in building an indigenous military capacity, and an assurance of assistance should India threaten the national security of Pakistan. All this not only upset the relative military strength between India and Pakistan but also completely offset the balance of power in the subcontinent.

Prior to the 1965 war, Lal Bahadur Shastri, the Indian Prime Minister, had protested at this excessive military aid by the US to Pakistan and expressed his apprehension that these weapons would be used against India. Subsequent events proved this to be true, despite an earlier assurance in writing from the Pakistani Prime Minister, Mohammed Ali, to Jawaharlal Nehru, that American arms would not be used against India.

The American President, General Dwight D. Eisenhower, had also sent a message to Prime Minister Nehru that stated:

. . . and I am confirming publicly that if our aid to any country, including Pakistan, is misused and is directed against another in aggression, I will undertake immediately, in accordance with my constitutional authority, appropriate action both within and without the United Nations to thwart such aggression.[2]

Future events were to prove that neither would Pakistan abide by its promise, nor would the US stand by the commitment made by its own President.

Meanwhile, Field Marshal Ayub Khan felt that he needed to do something spectacular to strengthen his power base and improve his sagging image. He was of the opinion that the capture of the state of Jammu and Kashmir would be a step in the right direction to seal his position as President of Pakistan. He consulted his corps commanders and they agreed with him, that this was the best time to annex the state of J & K. Ayub, who was also the army chief, directed Pakistan Army Headquarters to draw up a foolproof plan to achieve his aim.

Pakistani planners, after due deliberation, presented their strategy to the President. It consisted of three offensives following sequentially. These were code-named 'Operation Desert Hawk', 'Operation Gibraltar' and 'Operation Grand Slam'.

Operation Desert Hawk

This operation sought to take a measure of India by launching a limited offensive in the desert area of the

Rann of Kutch. Pakistan felt that this operation would give her the ability to test the calibre and will of the Government of India under the leadership of Lal Bahadur Shastri, draw India's attention away from the issue of J & K and use the opportunity to test the recently acquired weapons from the US.

On 6 April 1965, President Ayub Khan tasked General Tikka Khan to launch an offensive on Indian positions in the vicinity of Kanjarkot in the Rann of Kutch, and to capture Sardar Post by 9 April. It was this operation that was given the code name Operation Desert Hawk by Pakistan.

Operation Gibraltar

Operation Gibraltar was based on the strategy of guerrilla warfare. Pakistan planned to infiltrate a force of over 12,000 guerrillas into the hinterland of the state of J & K from Kargil in the north, to Kalidhar in the south. They were tasked with attacking state headquarters and destroying bridges, lines of communication and dumps of fuel, ammunition and supplies to generally create chaos in the rear areas and with instigating a revolt among the civilians of the state. They then planned to broadcast to the world that this was an insurrection against India by the people of J and K. Unfortunately, neither our central intelligence agencies nor our Army's intelligence organizations were able to pick up any hint of this impending guerrilla operation.

To stop further infiltration and to cut off those who had come across, a series of operations were launched by the Indian Army to secure the enemy guerrilla bases and routes of infiltration in the Kargil, Srinagar and Tithwal sectors.[3] The major operation was the one that secured the Haji Pir pass and the Haji Pir bulge, as this provided main access of ingress into the Kashmir Valley.[4]

Operation Grand Slam

Pakistan presumed that with the success of Operation Gibraltar, the state government of J & K would collapse, after which, Pakistani regular forces would launch Operation Grand Slam. They believed that the Indian Army defences in the area of Akhnur would be sandwiched and destroyed by a Pakistan Army offensive from the front and the Pakistani guerrillas and the civilian insurrectionists from the rear. As plans go, the strategy had merit, but things do not always go according to plan.

Kutch, April–May 1965

The Rann of Kutch is a salt-covered desert about 23,309 sq. km in area. The border there between India and Pakistan was in dispute, with Pakistan claiming about 9000 sq. km of the Rann as their territory on the basis that the Rann was a derelict seabed and that in accordance with maritime law, the international border should pass halfway through it. This plea of Pakistan was disproved by India, but Pakistan continued to keep the issue alive. The area had, however, never been physically contested and India had only police posts along the border to prevent cross-border smuggling. In January 1965, Indian police patrols discovered that Pakistan had constructed a track about 2 km inside Indian territory. Protests drew no response and this led to the Central Reserve Police Force being deployed forward and 31 Infantry Brigade of the Indian Army was moved forward from Dhrangadhra to Bhuj.[5]

Pakistan commenced Operation Desert Hawk by attacking Sardar Post on 9 April 1965 with an infantry brigade supported by artillery and quickly overran it. The Indian Army was now ordered to take care of the situation. The Para Brigade was moved forward and by 18 April, Kilo Sector was raised under Major General P.O. Dunn. By 22 April, Pakistan had moved its 8 Infantry Division and two armoured regiments forward and launched a divisional-sized attack under Major General Tikka Khan, supported by her newly acquired Patton tanks.

Indian forces were ordered to fight delaying actions against this oversized force and not to get involved in a major operation. A spirited resistance by the outnumbered and outgunned Indian defenders failed to convince a belligerent Pakistan that there was a need to deviate from her predisposed aggressive agenda. The Indian forces, after inflicting heavy casualties, pulled back as planned.

Indian formations were moved forward to their operational areas on 28 April 1965. A reconnaissance flight by Flying Officer Utpal Barbara in a Vampire confirmed without any doubt that Pakistan was using American-aided Pattons against India, which was against the assurances by the Pakistani Prime Minister and the American President to India. Flying Officer Barbara, along with his wingman, made six runs over the column of Pattons, taking close-up photographs of the tanks. These photographs were flown the same day to Delhi.

India had not responded with full force in order not to enlarge the conflict into a full-blown war. However, in a speech in the Lok Sabha on 28 April, Prime Minister Lal Bahadur Shastri sounded a warning to Pakistan that the conflict could spread. He stated that:

> India was quite prepared to find a peaceful solution to the problem provided that the status quo was restored. However, if Pakistan discards reason and persists in its aggressive activities, the Indian Army will implement its own strategy and the employment of its own manpower and equipment in the manner it deems best.[6]

The Indian Prime Minister protested to America against the use of American arms and equipment against India. America admonished Pakistan. That was as far as the assurance of an American President went, that arms supplied by her would not be used against India. Utpal Barbara's photographs of the Patton tanks were released to the Press Trust of India and to newspapers around the world. This showed that US-supplied equipment ostensibly meant to contain communism, was, in fact, being used against India in the Rann of Kutch.[7] This made little difference to Pakistan or the US as they were aware that they were going back on their own assurances that American arms would never be used against India.

Utpal Barbara's photographic reconnaissance that exposed Pakistan's use of American aid against India

(Source: https://threadreaderapp.com/thread/1098594936218357762.html)

However, the statement of the Indian Prime Minister and the general mobilization ordered in Punjab that commenced Operation Ablaze (India's response to Pakistan's Operation Desert Hawk), seemed to have unnerved Ayub Khan. Having convinced himself that he had achieved all his aims, he agreed to a ceasefire demanded by the UN and on 7 May 1965, ordered his forces to cease offensive action, while at the same time, he began preparing for a much bigger offensive in J & K. India continued to remain oblivious of Pakistan's devious plans and intentions.

The ceasefire agreement on cessation of incursions in the Rann of Kutch was brokered by the British

Prime Minister Harold Wilson and signed by India and Pakistan on 30 June 1965. The agreement was to be followed by an examination of the issue by a three-man tribunal. This apparently convinced India that Pakistan would follow the terms of the ceasefire agreement. India ought to have known better and should have looked at Pakistan's legacy of duplicity. Whilst ostensibly preparing to agree to the ceasefire, Pakistan initiated a series of violent incidents across the Cease-Fire Line (CFL) in J & K in preparation for her next offensive. In the month of May, there were 1345 incidents along the CFL in J & K, engineered by Pakistan and confirmed by UN observers.

In this matter, a warning came from an unexpected source. Shiv Kunal Verma in his book *1965: A Western Sunrise* states that the diplomatic back-and-forth continued for two months, but there were indications that trouble could well be brewing elsewhere. He quotes Ambassador M.K. Rasgotra,

> I was a war book officer at that time and an American embassy officer rang me up in the morning and asked for an urgent meeting. He said to me, 'Why are you people sending troops to Kutch? This is a sham attack to divert your attention from the north. Pakistan Army has been painting its war paint on its tanks. This is a diversionary tactic and a bigger attack is planned in the north.' I wrote up a note and sent it to the concerned authorities who took it seriously since I had known that this source was authentic. I think that the Americans were warning us. We took this threat seriously.

The ceasefire in the Rann of Kutch was followed by the Commonwealth Prime Ministers' Conference at London. An informal meeting took place on the sidelines of this conference between President Ayub Khan of Pakistan and the Indian Prime Minister Lal Bahadur Shastri. L.K. Jha, principal secretary to the Prime Minister, recalls:

> In fact, I recall, and it might be useful for the record, a meeting between Prime Minister Shastri and President Ayub during the Commonwealth Conference session. It was a private meeting and I was there. Ayub said somewhat patronisingly, 'You know, your chaps tried to commit aggression on our territory. Our chaps gave them a few knocks and they began to flee.' Then Shastriji said, 'Mr. President, you are a general. I have no military knowledge or experience. But do you think if I had to attack Pakistan, I would choose a terrain where we have no logistic support and you have all the advantages? Do you think I would make such a mistake?' And one could see from the face of President Ayub that this thought startled him. Because, quite obviously, he had been led to believe, in my judgement by Bhutto, that the Indians had attacked in the Rann of Kutch and he was firmly of that view until this question was posed by Shastriji. I could see him visibly pause and not pursue the point any further.[8]

Pakistan, however, learnt all the wrong lessons from this conflict. It believed that the Indian Government did not have the stomach for a fight, and that its own troops had mastered the use of the newly acquired weapons from

America. This strengthened its resolve to carry on with planned operations in Jammu and Kashmir and it moved forward to implement Operation Gibraltar. India, on the other hand, accepted the peace agreement in good faith, but the Kutch encounter created doubts in the minds of Indian planners about Pakistani intentions. The Indian Prime Minister announced publicly in Parliament that any attack on the state of J & K would be considered an attack on India and retaliation would be at a time and place of India's choosing.

Kashmir—Operation Gibraltar

The core of the force for Operation Gibraltar was drawn from the so-called Azad Kashmir Army, which was an integral part of the Pakistan Army. These regulars were supplemented by *razakars* (irregular soldiers) and mujahideen (religious warriors). This force was organized into ten columns under the overall command of Major General Akhtar Hussain Malik, GOC Pak 12 Infantry Division, and infiltrated across the CFL on a wide front between 2 and 5 August. Operations were supported by artillery from across the CFL. The enemy achieved complete surprise. Indian Central intelligence agencies and the Army's own intelligence had not picked up any indication of this operation. The infiltrators were able to close in on Srinagar and Gulmarg and other rear areas of J & K.

The success of Operation Gibraltar banked on the ability of the guerrillas to create an uprising by the civilians of J & K. In this, they failed completely. In fact, in many cases, the civilians actively helped the Indian forces.

The guerrillas were hunted down and destroyed and those who survived exfiltrated back into Pakistan-held areas. To cut off further infiltration and those who had come across, the Indian Army launched a series of operations to secure Pakistani bases and routes of infiltration. In the Tithwal sector, the Pir Sahiba feature was captured and Indian troops advanced up to the Kishanganga. Haji Pir was captured in a daring operation, effectively blocking infiltration along the main routes of ingress into the Kashmir Valley. By 21 August, the infiltration by the Pakistani guerrillas was crushed and the last remnants of the guerrilla force retreated into Pakistan after suffering heavy casualties.

Pakistan, as usual, denied complicity. Clear evidence of Pakistani involvement, however, was available and was reported as such by the UN military observers and by U Thant, the Secretary General of the UN, at the Security Council on 3 September 1965. Interrogation of captured Pakistani guerrillas revealed that Field Marshal Ayub Khan had himself addressed the guerrilla force commanders at Murree in July 1965, a month after Pakistan had signed the Kutch Peace Agreement that stated it would not resort to force to solve outstanding disputes.[9] So much for trusting Pakistani promises! The fall of Haji Pir and Indian successes in other areas along the CFL unnerved the Pakistanis. Instead of securing the Kashmir Valley, they were now in danger of losing parts of their illegally occupied portions of J & K.

Operation Grand Slam

Pakistan now put into effect Operation Grand Slam towards Chhamb and Akhnur. The attack was launched by their 12 Infantry Division with two infantry brigades, two armoured regiments from 6 Armoured Division supported by their full complement of Division and Corps artillery that included medium and heavy artillery. Two more infantry brigades from 7 Infantry Division were to be used subsequently. Operation Grand Slam was launched on 1 September 1965 with an intense artillery bombardment of the defended area of 191 Indian Infantry Brigade which had only three infantry battalions in the plains sector and an infantry battalion in the hill sector. Once again, the Pakistanis achieved complete surprise and by the evening of that day, the Pakistanis had reached the Munawar Tawi River. 191 Infantry Brigade fought a strong defensive battle but could not do much against the overwhelming strength of the Pakistani assault. During the night, it fell back through 41 Mountain Brigade, which had arrived as reinforcements and had taken up defences at Troti Heights between Jaurian and Akhnur.

Although some preliminary planning, including anticipation of the enemy's axes of advance into Chhamb and the pattern of our defensive action had been made, Indian planners had failed to implement our counter-offensive plans on the ground and the rapid progress of the Pakistani offensive had caught Indian planners at short notice. The enemy had an edge over us in armour, infantry and artillery. Basically, our force for the defence of the Chhamb battleground was inadequate and for this, there is no excuse because this contingency had been war-gamed but not acted upon.[10]

Meanwhile, there was a change of command in the Pakistani side from 12 Infantry Division to 7 Infantry Division and Yahya Khan took over from Akhtar Hussain Malik at Jaurian. This resulted in a twenty-four-hour pause that broke the momentum of the Pakistani attack, allowing India's 41 Mountain Brigade to fall back for the defence of Akhnur along with 191 Infantry Brigade.

Rumours in Pakistan had it that the Pakistan Army hierarchy did not want the success of this operation to be attributed to Maj. Gen. A.H. Malik, who was an Ahmediya, and instead wanted the credit to be given to Maj. Gen. Yahya Khan—a Pathan. The delay in the handing-taking over of Operation Grand Slam helped Indian defenders to reorganize and take position on a more defensible line. It was at this stage that Prime Minister Shastri took the decision to open a second front in Punjab across the international border. This forced the Pakistanis on 6 September to call off Operation Grand Slam and hurriedly withdraw her forces to face the new threat across the international border in Punjab. During these operations, the Indian Air Force was employed for the first time with air strikes being used against Pakistani armour on 1 September and subsequent days.

The fighting now shifted from Jammu and Kashmir to Punjab.

Punjab Khem Karan and Asal Uttar

At that time, Northern Command did not exist and the whole area from Ladakh to the border of Rajasthan came under Western Command, with Lieutenant General Harbakhsh Singh as the Western Army Commander. General Harbakhsh ordered 121 Infantry Brigade Group which was deployed in the Kargil Sector to evict Pakistani intruders from Pt. 13620 and Black Rocks that were overlooking the Srinagar-Leh highway. This was carried out by 17–18 May 1965. General J.N. Chaudhuri, the Indian Army Chief, was in Kashmir on 1 September when the Pakistani offensive on Chhamb commenced. He immediately flew back to Delhi and, with the consent of the Prime Minister, issued orders for opening the offensive into Punjab. The plan involved XI Corps to advance to the east bank of the Ichhogil Canal from opposite Amritsar to opposite Khem Karan, and for I Corps to launch an offensive from Samba towards Sialkot.[11]

It was decided to open the Lahore front with XI Corps a few days prior to the offensive against Sialkot, in order to draw the enemy offensive forces away from Chhamb and give India's recently raised I Corps and its 1 Armoured Division sufficient time to move towards the Sialkot Sector.

In accordance with our plans to cross the border in areas of our choosing, three divisions—4, 15 and 7 of XI Corps—advanced simultaneously across the international border. To maintain surprise, assaulting troops advanced directly from their peacetime locations to their assembly areas during the night of 5/6 September and crossed the international border at dawn of 6 September. Complete surprise was achieved, which resulted in a series of successes in the initial operations.

In the Lahore Sector, Pakistan's defences were based on the Ichhogil Canal. Built after 1947, this canal, although constructed as an irrigation project, was fashioned as a defence obstacle with concrete pillboxes along its brick-lined banks. The tasks given to XI Corps was to secure the Ichhogil Canal, establish bridgeheads across it and pose a threat to Lahore.

It was expected that Pakistan forces would react violently and provide XI Corps the opportunity to destroy them. It was decided that Asal Uttar would be a better place to cover an enemy offensive rather than Khem Karan, which could be bypassed. Asal Uttar covered both the Khem Karan–Patti axis and the Khem Karan–Amritsar axis. Defending Lahore were Pakistan's 10 Infantry Division in a defensive role and 11 Infantry Division in offensive defence. Pakistan's 1 Armoured Division was located behind Pakistan's 11 Infantry Division, allowing it to team up with this division to form a strike corps[12] and launch an offensive through Khem Karan and then head for Amritsar and the Beas River.

On the 15 Division front, 3 Jat of 54 Infantry Brigade led the advance along the GT Road. The battalion achieved complete surprise and, supported by a troop of 14 Horse, moved forward and crossed the Ichhogil Canal, captured Dograi and advanced towards Lahore reaching the Batapore area on its outskirts. However, the supporting arms and the rest of the brigade could not keep up with 3 Jat, and without artillery support and ancillary arms, the battalion was out on a limb and they had to be recalled. 3 Jat considered this to be an insult to their regimental pride and subsequently recaptured Dograi. The Jat attack is a saga of courage. The battalion fought courageously under the leadership of Lieutenant Colonel Desmond Hayde. The ferocity of the fighting can be gauged by the fact that the Jats suffered 216 casualties, including ten officers. From that area, 840 Pakistani bodies were recovered.

India's decision to open a second front in Punjab took Pakistan by surprise and they were compelled to withdraw forces that were poised to continue their offensive to take Akhnur. The change of command of the Pakistani offensive forces that had taken place earlier had disturbed the momentum of their offensive, and allowed our forces to reorganize for the defence of Akhnur. The opportunity for Pakistan to take Akhnur was lost.

The Pakistani concern about the Indian offensive by I Corps in the area of Shakargarh and XI Corp's offensive towards Lahore resulted in a counter-offensive by Pakistan to head for Amritsar and the Beas. Indian forces on the ground redeployed to destroy this offensive.

Between 7 and 10 September, the Pakistani Armoured Brigades attacked exactly as anticipated and attempted to break through our defensive positions. First, they tried to overrun the 4 Grenadiers position. This battalion held out with great determination and gallantry against heavy pressure from the enemy and succeeded in destroying several Pakistani Patton tanks. CQMH Abdul Hamid was the architect of the destruction of enemy armour in front of his battalion-defended area by destroying seven Pakistani Patton tanks. He was eventually killed in the process and was awarded the Param Vir Chakra posthumously for his courage and leadership on the battlefield.

Unknown to XI Corps, the Indian 4 Infantry Division had broken into the enemy's axis of ingress. Pakistan's 1 Armoured Division and 11 Infantry Division had concentrated at Kasur to launch a major offensive into India. The attack by 4 Indian Infantry Division inadvertently turned into a spoiling attack and delayed the Pakistani offensive by twenty-four hours. This delay proved vital for 4 Infantry Division to enable it to organize its defences and for 2 Indian Independent Armoured Brigade to deploy in the area. Between 8 and 10 September, the enemy made many efforts to break through the Indian defences but failed. From an armour-infantry battle, the fight now developed into an armoured battle between Pakistan's 1 Armoured Division with four regiments of Pattons and one Chaffee Regiment and India's 2 Independent Armoured Brigade with two Sherman and one Centurion Regiment. Though the Pakistanis were superior in armour, they were unable to make any headway and suffered tremendous losses at Khem Karan and Asal Uttar. A total of ninety-seven tanks were lost by Pakistan in this area. Our troops captured thirty-two tanks in good running condition. The General Officer Commanding Pakistan's 1 Armoured Division barely escaped capture by soldiers of 4 Grenadiers, and the Commander Artillery of the division was killed within the battalion-defended area of this gallant unit.

The Pakistani offensive ground to a halt and having lost the ability to continue any further, Pakistan called off its offensive and pulled out the remnants of her 1 Armoured Division to meet India's I Corps offensive in the north.

The offensive of India's I Corps into the Sialkot zone was intended to counter Pakistan's thrust into Chhamb where it was trying to capture Akhnur Bridge. I Corps had been raised on 1 April 1965, a few months before the war. It had on its ORBAT, 1 Armoured Division, 6 Mountain Division, 14 Infantry Division and 26 Infantry Division. Of these, 14 Infantry Division, like Headquarters I Corps, had also just been raised on 1 April 1965 and 6 Mountain Division had not been equipped or trained for fighting in the plains.

The I Corps offensive started on 8 September 1965. 6 and 26 Divisions secured their initial objectives, but 1 Armoured Division took time to secure Phillora and Pagowal, allowing the enemy to build up and strengthen its defences with armour and infantry. Phillora was contacted on 10 September and the attack was launched on 11 September. There now took place another big tank battle, nearly as big as the one fought at Khem Karan and Asal Uttar. After a fierce fight, the enemy withdrew and Phillora was finally captured by 6 Indian Infantry Division on 13 September. The next objective was Chawinda, 5 km from Phillora. From 14 September onwards, several attacks were launched but met with fierce resistance. During the battle of Phillora, Lieutenant Colonel Adi Tarapore, the Commanding Officer of Poona Horse, was fatally wounded and succumbed to his injuries. For his outstanding leadership and courage, he was awarded the Param Vir Chakra, India's highest award for courage on the battlefield.

The United Nations had been endeavouring to ensure a ceasefire for some time, but Pakistan kept insisting that a ceasefire must be accompanied by a solution to the Kashmir question, including an internationally supervised plebiscite. India accepted the UN's demand but without any preconditions. The ceasefire finally came into effect on 23 September without any preconditions.

The Indian Navy and Its Part in the 1965 War

The Indian Navy was not allowed to participate in the Indo–Pak war of 1965. This needs to be placed in the proper perspective. In addition to the economic and military aid that Pakistan received from the US, it also received substantial aid in terms of naval equipment, which included five destroyers, two of which were modern battle-class destroyers, and eight minesweepers. It also had a fleet of Scorpene submarines—the best submarine, at that time, in the world. The imbalance further increased when Indonesia, after the Sino–Indian war of 1962, began to take a pro-Pakistan stance. She distanced herself from India and moved closer to Pakistan. The expansion of her naval fleet with the help of the Soviet Union further increased the Indonesian Navy's confidence. Her bellicosity grew and she began to voice claims on some of the Nicobar Islands. Suggestions were also made by her that the Indian Ocean should be renamed as the Indonesian Ocean. There was an increase in the sightings of unidentified submarines and aircraft around the Andaman and Nicobar Islands. In response to Pakistan's request for assistance, the Indonesian Navy sent two submarines and two missile boats to Karachi. Indonesian strategy appeared to get Pakistan to tie down the Indian Navy on the western seaboard so that she could have easier access to capture some of our island territories of the Nicobar chain. In consequence, the Indian Navy had to send a considerable part of its fleet to the Bay of Bengal. Air Marshal Asghar Khan of Pakistan in his memoirs, *The First Round*, recounts his discussion with President Sukarno and Admiral Martadinata of Indonesia:

> President Sukarno said that India's attack on Pakistan was like an attack on Indonesia and they were duty bound to give Pakistan all possible assistance. President Soekarno told me to take away whatever would be useful to Pakistan in this emergency. Two Russian supplied submarines and two Russian supplied missile boats were sent to Pakistan post haste.

Admiral Martadinata asked Air Marshal Asghar Khan:

> Don't you want us to take over the Andaman Islands? A look at the map will show that the Andaman Islands are an extension of Sumatra and are in any case between East Pakistan and Indonesia. What right have the Indians to be there? In any case the Indonesian Navy will immediately commence patrols of the approaches to these islands and carry out reconnaissance missions to see what the Indians have there.[13]

Unfortunately for Indonesia and Pakistan, by the time the Indonesian ships and submarines reached Karachi, the war was wrapped up and over.

As soon as the Indo–Pak war of 1965 had shifted from the territory of J & K to areas across the international border in Punjab, the complexion of the war shifted from being a localized one restricted to J & K, to an all-out war across all borders and involving all the three services.

While the Indian Army and the Air Force were already fighting the war, the Navy felt that there was now an opportunity to also use the Navy to augment the war effort. However, due to the deployment of the greater portion of the Indian naval fleet in the Bay of Bengal, to counter the threat from Indonesia, the Government of India kept the Indian Navy out of the war. A government directive was sent by an official of the ministry of defence that in order not to widen the war, the Indian Navy was not to proceed more than 200 nautical miles beyond Bombay nor north of the parallel of Porbandar.[14] This effectually kept the Navy from launching any offensive operations in the Arabian Sea. This greatly upset Admiral Bhaskar Sadashiv Soman, the Naval Chief, who asked to see Shri Y.B. Chavan, the Raksha Mantri (Defence Minister).

The Raksha Mantri met the Naval Chief and informed him that the matter had been considered in detail and that he was sorry the Navy had been overlooked since the Sino-Indian war of 1962 and that as such, it would perhaps be better if the Navy did not go looking for trouble. Admiral Soman then gave out his reasons why the Navy should not be left out of battle.

The Raksha Mantri replied that in accordance with the government's order of priorities, the responsibilities assigned to the Navy for the defence of the Andaman and Nicobar Islands against a possible attack from Indonesia was more crucial than naval operations against Pakistan. The non-availability of INS *Vikrant*, which was in dry dock, also needed to be considered and it was the opinion of the Prime Minister that the Navy should not escalate the situation.

The Naval Chief then asked to meet with the Prime Minister. This too was organized and the Naval Chief met the Prime Minister the next morning. Admiral Soman describes his interview with the Prime Minister, saying:

> When I called on the Prime Minister, he brought up the same two points—the Navy had not been strengthened since the Sino-Indian conflict and its responsibilities in the Andaman and Nicobar area were more important than in the Arabian Sea. The Prime Minister brought up the undesirability of escalating the war at sea. I then brought out some historical examples to vindicate my point. This seemed to annoy the Prime Minister who said. 'You have no choice.' I asked him whether he had any objection to my seeing the Supreme Commander of the Armed Forces, meaning the President. The Prime Minister smiled and politely said, 'No, you do not have to see him.[15]

Excerpts from the recollections of government officials, as given in *Transition to Triumph: The Story of the Indian Navy*

1965-1975 probably better describe the circumstances that determined the government's thinking at that time. L.K. Jha, then Principal Secretary to the Prime Minister, recollects:

> Admiral Soman had in the meantime—ever since the involvement of the Air Force been straining at the leash, saying 'Look, let me go into action.' But again, the same consideration, which was acting as a restraint on using the Air Force or going into Lahore prevailed. It was felt if we now opened another front off Karachi; it would become a major engagement and would no longer be a matter of a localised conflict. So, the decision was taken that the operation to march to Lahore would be launched but that the Navy would not be involved.
>
> The Indian Army crossed the international border at Wagah on the morning of 6 September and headed for Lahore. President Ayub went on the air. It was a very, very strong and angry broadcast. Admiral Soman thought that the opening of the Lahore front meant that a no-holds-barred situation had come and he, I think, issued a signal that we were at war with Pakistan. This signal had to be countermanded because we did not want to go to that stage so soon. But still we felt that the Navy had the capability and if the event so necessitated, I don't think there would have been too long a hesitation to use it. But the feeling was strong that if we could contain the Pakistani forces and hold them on land, then it would perhaps be wiser not to get the Navy involved. I knew that the Navy was not happy with this decision because they were very anxious to get into action.

The prevalent orders at that time prevented the Navy from contributing usefully to the war and permitted the Pakistan Navy to bombard the coast of Gujarat with impunity. Although this had no effect on military operations, it gave the Pakistan Navy a boost in morale and this was seen by them as a humiliation of India and her Navy. Civilians and officers of the armed forces asked why the Indian Navy could not do anything in retaliation to Pakistan's raid on Dwarka and the reputation of the Navy plummeted. Few knew that all this was because of a diktat from the government.[16]

Strangely, the Pakistani submarine PNS *Ghazi* claimed that it had sunk the Indian frigate INS *Brahmaputra* and three gallantry awards were announced by Islamabad. The Pakistan Naval Chief was awarded the Hilal-i-Jurat; Commander K.R. Niazi, Commanding Officer, PNS *Ghazi*, and his second-in-command Tasnim Ahmed were both awarded the Sitara-i-Jurat. An engine room artificer G. Nabi was awarded the Tamgha-i-Jurat.[17] However, the Indian Navy and the *Brahmaputra* were totally unaware of an underwater attack or any type of attack on it, and along with all other frigates, it was paraded at Bombay to satisfy the media that this episode was entirely a figment of Pakistan's imagination.

The Navy did operate in the Arabian Sea but strictly within the boundaries of the directive given by the Ministry of Defence. It is unfortunate that the Ministry of Defence did not make a statement that it was on its directions that the Navy had to play a purely defensive role in the 1965 war. In the ultimate analysis, however, the passive role played by the Navy in the 1965 war, and the repercussions it caused within the Navy, had a useful outcome, as this was the prime factor that motivated the Navy and senior naval officers like Admiral Nanda to make sure that the Navy played its rightful role in the war of 1971 to carve out a spectacular victory both in the Arabian Sea and the Bay of Bengal.

The Air War

While the battles between the land armies of India and Pakistan raged on the ground, their air counterparts battled it out to take control of the sky. The Pakistan Air Force (PAF) used F-86 Sabre jets, F-104 Starfighters and B-57 Canberras while the Indian Air Force (IAF) used Hunters, Gnats and Mirages—a mixed bag of aircraft from different countries of the world. The stories that follow include one of Alfred Cooke, the IAF pilot who single-handedly took on 4 Pakistani Sabre jets, destroying two and getting one more in his sights only to find that he had run out of ammunition. A story that is not included in this book is the one about Tubby Devayya who shot down a supersonic F-104 Starfighter with a subsonic Mirage narrated in the book *Beyond Fear* published in 2023—an inspiring story, not only for the amazing fight between two unequal fighter planes but also because Tubby was awarded a Maha Vir Chakra twenty-three years after the event.[18]

Prior to the 1965 war, during the Kutch skirmish, Flying Officer Utpal Barbara flying a Vampire low over Pakistani forces confirmed the use of American Patton tanks being used in violation of the agreement between Pakistan, the US and India. During Operation Gibraltar, the role of the PAF was limited to the use of transport aircraft and helicopters. However, during Operation Grand Slam, the limited war in J & K progressed into an all-out war with no holds barred.

The use of old, antiquated Vampires in the battle of Chhamb against far superior F-86 Sabre jets was a regrettable mistake as they were just shot out of the sky. Notwithstanding the inequality in calibre to the opposing side's aircraft, the IAF pilots bravely took to the sky in defence of the country and bravely suffered the consequences—a sacrifice of pilots and aircraft that was unnecessary and a loss that is unacceptable.

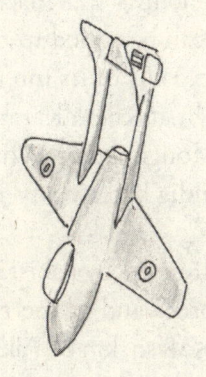

The obsolete Vampire

P.V.S. Jagan Mohan and Samir Chopra have extensively covered the air aspect of the 1965 Indo–Pak war in their book *The India–Pakistan Air War of 1965*. The book not only brings out the details of aerial combat between the rival air forces during the war but also about ground strike missions, aerial bombing and raids into rival territories It features the evolution of the two air forces before and after Partition in 1947 and the characteristics of the aircraft of the rival nations' air forces.

Conclusion

Whereas India and Pakistan both claim that they were victorious, one needs to consider that it was Pakistan who initiated the war with the express purpose of annexing the state of J & K by force. It failed to do so. Also, military strategists consider that victory can be claimed by the side which destroys the enemy's war machine. Destruction of the enemy's armour can be added to the fact that Pakistan was not able to achieve any of its intended objectives. The two tank battles fought at Khem Karan and Phillora are the greatest tank battles fought since World War II. Pakistan lost 170 tanks and India had twenty-nine tanks destroyed and forty damaged.

Every planned offensive by Pakistan was neutralized by the Indian armed forces and at the time of the ceasefire, India had captured 1528 sq. km of Pakistani territory while Pakistan held about 554 sq. km of Indian territory. This should be an indicator of which side got the better of its opponent and who won the war.

The ceasefire, however, led to an uneasy peace and firing continued to take place across the CFL. Prime Minister Kosygin of the Soviet Union offered to mediate and invited the leaders of both countries to meet at Tashkent on 4 January 1966. Both sides were persuaded to give up all areas captured during the war and to return to the status quo as it existed prior to 5 August 1965, i.e., the start of Pakistani infiltration into Jammu and Kashmir. This meant that India had to give up all areas captured including the Haji Pir pass and Pakistan had to withdraw from the areas across Chhamb and from Jaurian.

As far as the Indian Army was concerned, major weaknesses in the equipment profile of the army surfaced. This included the quality and quantity of our tanks, radio equipment, artillery, anti-aircraft guns and a host of other items. A reappraisal of all weapons and equipment was undertaken. The raising of new units and formations were ordered. The 1965 war had brought out clearly the need of better compatibility between armour and infantry, resulting in steps to obtain armoured personnel carriers which resulted in the raising of mechanized infantry regiments. The war also brought out the gap in Army–Air Force cooperation and the need for better jointmanship. Methods in both individual and collective training were revised. This resulted in raising the profile of the Indian Army.[19]

Unfortunately, Prime Minister Lal Bahadur Shastri passed away at Tashkent.

The Tashkent Agreement brought Pakistan to 'square one' and Ayub Khan returned to Pakistan as a chastened head of state, having failed to achieve any of his planned objectives. This led to his eventual overthrow.

I

Combat above Kharagpur

'Life is an exciting business and most exciting when it is lived for others.'

—Helen Keller

7 September 1965, 1025 hours, IIT Kharagpur

It was just a few minutes before the scheduled tea break at the Indian Institute of Technology (IIT) Kharagpur, when a series of explosions outside the institute rattled the windows of all the buildings. The continuing roar of strange sounds made it difficult for the professors to hold the attention of their students. Unable to restrain the curiosity about what was happening outside, the professors closed their classes and students and professors together streamed out of the institute to see what the noise was all about. What they saw was astonishing! Fighter planes were criss-crossing the sky, their silver bodies glistening in the late morning sun as they twisted, turned and rolled over in their attempts to destroy one another.

The war with Pakistan was a week old and the sound of the cannons of the opposing fighter planes told them that this was the 'real thing'. What they did not know was that they were witnessing one of the greatest air battles in the subcontinent.

Around this time, oblivious of what was happening on the ground and in the air, Raksha Mantri Shri Y.B. Chavan was drafting a message to Air Headquarters, not to escalate the war by launching operations into East Pakistan as he and Prime Minister Lal Bahadur Shastri felt that they had enough on their hands already, and they had no desire to extend the war into East Pakistan. The Raksha Mantri was a day too late, because Central Air Command had already given orders to attack Pakistani air bases at Chittagong, Kurmitola and other PAF airbases, unfortunately with no positive outcomes. On the contrary, these attacks precipitated a ferocious response from the Pakistani airbase at Tezgaon outside Dhaka, where Pakistan's 14 Squadron had a detachment of twelve Sabres.

2 September 1965, Tezgaon Airfield

Ghulam Haider (Nosey Haider), the Pakistani Station Commander at Tezgaon, had been informed as early as 2 September, that once the conflict started, he would be on his own. He was happy with this bit of information, because it meant that he could act without waiting for orders. Haider had submitted his plan to PAF headquarters before hostilities started. It was immediately approved with the clause that it could be put into action only after hostilities broke out in the west. The IAF attacks on Pakistani airbases at Kurmitola, Chittagong and others was just the opportunity Haider was looking for.

7 September 1965, Kalaikunda Airfield

At 0640 hours on 7 September, Indian Air Force personnel at Kalaikunda were just emerging for their day's activities when five Sabres pulled up over Kharagpur and dived in to attack the Kalaikunda airbase. India's Central Air Command was short on radar coverage and so no warning was received from outlying radar stations.[1] The Sabres kept low. Squadron Leader Shabbir Syed led the Sabres from the direction of the Bay of Bengal where no observation post (OP) could relay their approach.

Flight Lieutenants Haleem Basheer, Tariq Khan and Afzal Khan accompanied him on this mission. After take-off at 0600 hours, the formation carried out a 300 km flight over the sea. To cater for the long distance, the Sabres carried a full reserve of extra fuel in their drop tanks and left only with their 0.5 machine guns as their weaponry.

Kalaikunda was jolted out of its routine by the clatter of machine guns as the Sabres homed in for the kill. Only three ack-ack[2] guns were deployed as they had just arrived the previous day.

In the absence of any combat air patrol to oppose enemy strikes and aircraft being parked in the open at Kalaikunda, the IAF lost eight aircraft—four Canberras and four Vampires to Sabre strikes on 7 September 1965. The Pak response to the Indian attack had struck the

IAF hard. The massive Canberras already refuelled and re-armed were an attractive target for the attacking Sabres and the Canberras went up in flames. Four Vampires of 24 Squadron were lined up on the other side of the runway. These too were quickly destroyed. The Sabres returned to Tezgaon, making an exaggerated claim of fourteen Canberras destroyed and six others damaged, and four Hunters damaged.

Ghulam Haider's initial foray was entirely successful and he was looking forward to some more independent missions. This PAF raid was one of the most successful of the war and Haider was suitably decorated.

Overjoyed at the success of his planned mission, he made the mistake of executing a second mission to destroy whatever they had earlier missed out on. The pilots did not realize that Kalaikunda was now on full alert and they would be heading for trouble.

7 September, 0600 hours, Dum Dum Airfield

Early that morning, Flight Lieutenant (Flt Lt) Alfred Cooke and Flying Officer S.C. Mamgain had just returned from a dawn task to provide protection to Canberras from their airbase on a strike mission. Hardly had they sat down to a quick breakfast when they were once again scrambled to an alert from their radar station that two bogies[3] had appeared north of Dum Dum. The bogies were operating within their own border area at 25,000 ft. Cooke and Mamgain, who were flying Hunters, returned to their airbase at Dum Dum around 0900 hours after two fruitless missions. Little did they realize that an explosive air duel was waiting for them and they settled down to a twice-postponed breakfast. As they were about to start eating, Cooke and Mamgain were scrambled once again and vectored north of Dum Dum to approximately the same area covered by the previous sortie.

7 September, 1030 hours, Kalaikunda Airfield

At about 1030 hours, an alarm was raised at Kalaikunda warning of a second attack led by Flt Lt Haleem.

Squadron Leader 'Mama' Sahni, the radar officer at 55 Surveillance Unit (SU) at Kalaikunda, briefly picked up a blip on his scope near Fort Canning and immediately alerted Wing Commander 'Dicky' Law, OC Flying at Kalaikunda, of multiple enemy aircraft coming in for a second raid. Law looked around at his resources; two Hunters flown by Cooke and Mamgain were 60 miles north of Kalaikunda at 20,000 ft.

Cooke, a lanky 6'3" youngster, universally regarded as the squadron's 'top gun' air defence pilot, had grown up dreaming of being a fighter pilot as he watched Hurricanes, Spitfires, P-51 Mustangs and P-38 Lightnings tangling in mock battles near his childhood home at Agra. Now with 600 hours of flying Hunters to his credit, he was itching to get to grips with the enemy. His training included gruelling practice in low-level air combat with 'Piloo' Kacker, an innovative air force fighter pilot who had his own aggressive ideas of air combat. Kacker had defied IAF regulations in low-level combat flying. It would stand

Cooke in good stead for what lay ahead of him that day. The stage was set for one of the greatest air battles in the history of air combat in the subcontinent. The decisive moment had arrived!

On 7 September at daybreak, Cooke and Mamgain were tasked to cover their squadron commander, Denis Lafontaine, on a mission. After they returned, they received a scramble order and were vectored to an area 80 miles north of Dum Dum. They were informed that there were two bogies at 25,000 feet but were to engage with them only if they entered Indian air space. The enemy aircraft orbited on their side of the border and Cooke and Mamgain returned to base at around 0900 hours.

Meanwhile, as already mentioned, Kalaikunda had been attacked and a number of our aircraft had been destroyed on the ground.

At around 1000 hours, the pair were scrambled again and vectored to the same area covered by the previous sortie. They were also reminded not to engage unless the bogies crossed the international border (IB).

Cooke felt these were decoys and the real target was once again Kalaikunda. He radioed 411 SU controller and asked if there was any movement by enemy aircraft towards Kalaikunda. After a while, the SU controller excitedly informed him that he was right, and that the PAF aircraft were heading towards Kalaikunda and asked him whether he had enough fuel to intercept the PAF raiders. Cooke checked with Mamgain and both confirmed they had enough fuel, and Cooke asked for 'pigeons back to base'[4]. They were told they were approximately 120 nautical miles away and given a heading for Kalaikunda at 0.9 Mach (500 knots). Cooke, who was senior, told Mamgain that they would have to use all their skills to get the better of the enemy in the dogfight that lay ahead.

Cooke led both the Hunters into a shallow dive at 0.9 Mach towards KKD, calculating his speed and rate of descent so as to arrive 10 km short of KKD at 500 feet and aiming to keep above the Sabres. Once below 10,000 feet, they lost contact with 411 SU. They tried to contact KKD but received no response because the control tower at KKD was under attack.

On arrival over KKD, Cooke made visual contact with the Sabres. The Sabres were employed in a front gun classic racecourse pattern[5] of attack. As one Sabre kept top cover, three Sabres made their attack run on the western side of the runway while another kept cover on the eastern side.

Cooke's response was immediate. He called out to Mamgain, 'Look at those bastards! Let's get them. I'm taking on the three on this side—you break and take on the ones on the other side . . . good luck.'

Cooke was under the impression that there were six Sabres—three on either side of the runway. What he decided on was not in accordance with accepted teaching, because the wingman is supposed to stay glued to the leader's tail. But under these special circumstances, as this one was, Cooke decided that the best thing to do was to take a chance, split up and take three Sabres each.

Flt Lt Haleem was leading the Sabre formation, with Flt Lt Basheer as his wingman. Flt Lts Tariq Habib Khan and Afzal Khan were the second pair in the formation. One Sabre was on its strafing run when Cooke and Mamgain appeared on the scene. The Sabres outnumbered the Hunters two to one.

Cooke got behind one Sabre, fired at it and chased it so low that one could see the trees in his gun camera film. This Sabre was piloted by Afzal Khan in what became a classic dogfight employing scissors manoeuvres. Both aircraft tried to outdo each other, to get behind and on top of the other or to break away. Cooke, however, used his better acceleration and opened up with his 30 mm cannon, hitting the Sabre, which broke up in the air. Cooke flew through the debris damaging his aircraft in the process. Flt Lt Afzal Khan was killed. Some excerpts from Cooke's narrative from the moment of engagement to the kill make for exhilarating reading.

> . . . I knew then that these guys were going exactly as per the book and I knew chapter and verse of what they were doing. When his speed dropped off, he would dive down to build up speed and then start fighting again—pulling out of the dive at tree height (50 feet or less) with me following hoping I would 'mush' into the ground. I got my gun-sight on him when we were very low and took a shot at him. I started firing at him from a range of 600 yards and I could see that he was below tree-line height. I did not realise that I was that low and that my wing-tip was actually hitting the scrub. I stopped firing to get away from the ground and saw his aircraft explode into a ball of flame and I could not avoid flying through the fireball and the debris.[6]

The students and professors of IIT Kharagpur got a grandstand view of the roaring air battles above their institution and their homes. The students cheered loudly when the Sabres and the Hunters, one or the other, seemed to be at the receiving end. They had no idea of which aircraft belonged to which side—they were just applauding the spectacle of fighter aircraft engaged in a fight to the finish.

During the scissors, Cooke could clearly see Afzal's face and he still remembers that Afzal was wearing a white helmet just like his own. Khan's Sabre crashed near the IIT campus on a farmer's hut, killing two civilians.

Cooke thereafter got after the second Sabre which had attempted to get behind him and fired at it, damaging it severely. Large bits of the Sabre's wings were torn off as Cooke's bullets repeatedly found their mark. In his own words, Cooke describes how he chased and got the better of his second opponent:

> On recovering from this (Afzal Khan's kill) I took a quick look around and saw another Sabre behind me. I took violent evasive manoeuvres and during the criss-cross scissors we got very close to each other. I got into an advantageous position behind him and started firing while he was trying to get away from me by diving and turning towards the ground. (All this took place between ground level and about 4,000 feet.) While firing at him I noticed that he steepened his bank even more and something at the back of my mind warned me that he was being warned by another Sabre who could be behind me. I kept on firing and closing in rapidly on him and I could see pieces of his aircraft disintegrating. I stopped firing, as I was so close (100 yards) that if I did not break away, I would collide with him.

IAF Hunters getting into combat with PAF Sabre Jets over IIT Kharagpur, 7 September 1965, 1025 hrs

Cooke's second Sabre was almost certainly flown by Flt Lt Tariq Habib Khan. This Sabre, damaged by Cooke, managed to disengage and escape, and according to the PAF, was written off due to non-availability of spares. Other Sabres were around, including the one Cooke suspected was on his tail. Cooke continues:

'On recovering from this, I immediately pulled upward to the right and saw another Sabre behind me.

I out manoeuvred him and got behind him as he pulled up in a vertical climb and then winged over to go into a vertical dive with me following and firing at him all the time. In the vertical dive, I kept firing at him as he pulled out of the dive and moved away from me. I was mesmerised and so full of adrenaline that it took me some time to realise that I would fly into the ground unless I pulled out of the dive myself. I pulled back on the joystick and my finger on the trigger and got out of the dive with guns still firing until I had expended my ammunition.'

Meanwhile Mamgain went after the two remaining Sabres who immediately turned and engaged him. In the dogfight that followed, Mamgain hit one of the Sabres and claimed that he shot it down.

One down, two chased off. But one more Sabre was still around and Cooke's No. 2, Mamgain was in danger of being shot down before Cooke intervened. Cooke says: 'I was very shaken at this stage and I turned back towards the airfield to get my bearing and my equilibrium back. It was then that I noticed that my No. 2 Mamgain doing a leisurely turn at about 1,500 feet with a Sabre 1,500 yards behind him and closing in fast. I warned him and gave him a 'break port[7]' and took on this Sabre also.'

Cooke managed to get on top of and behind this Sabre also. He had him in his sights and pressed the trigger of his cannons but nothing happened. He now realized that he had expended all his ammunition. Cooke would have been justified in breaking away from combat at this stage because he was out of ammunition but he knew that the Sabre did not know that and stuck to him anyhow. The Sabre tried every trick he knew to get away from Cooke's relentless chase. The unnerved Pak pilot finally disengaged, started climbing and headed towards East Pakistan. Cooke followed about 3000 yards behind. The chase took Cooke all the way to the border and then he finally decided to return to Dum Dum.

Cooke's adventures had not ended. After he managed to get away from our own anti-aircraft fire, he looked around and found that he had sustained some damage to his portside wing tip and saw that the pitot tube[8] was bent to about 70 degrees. This meant that he had no air speed indicator and so he asked 411 SU to get some Hunters to shepherd him in. 411 SU could not contact Dum Dum so Cooke told them that he was coming in on an emergency landing. ATC informed Cooke that there was a Pan Am 707 on long finals.[9]

This failed to impress Cooke, who insisted that he was very low on fuel, and he cut in, in front of the Boeing to put his Hunter on the runway. He was at excessive speed and had to use his tail chute. With heavy braking, he managed just in time to turn into his taxi track seconds before the Pan Am 707 thundered past. Cooke's engine cut off just 600 yards from the parking area. His Hunter was out of fuel!

A day of action like no other had come to an end.

Postscript

Later in the evening, the squadron looked at Alfred Cooke's gun film. It showed bits and pieces of the Sabre flying off and trees scraping the wingtips of Cooke's Hunter. Wing Commander Lafontaine, the squadron commander, exclaimed, 'Alfred, you fired at four different Sabres!' 'I didn't know that, Sir!' replied Cooke.

The battle had been fought at a frightening low level and often at dangerously close range. It had seen one pilot take on four different Sabres and fight them in contrasting styles. His mastery of the Hunter and his ability to exploit its strengths against a formidable adversary like the Sabre had seen him emerge triumphant. His gun camera showed that he had fired against all four Sabres and hit three. One got hit and broke up. The second was badly damaged and the third was also damaged but escaped. A police station near the border reported a lone jet aircraft coming low trailing smoke and the pilot ejecting just across the border. Radio intercepts also reported ejects due to low fuel situations of the Sabres. Mamgain's gun camera evidence was inconclusive, but given Group Captain Law's report of two Sabres downed, he was given credit of a Sabre kill.

Years later, PAF admitted the loss of another Sabre which was too badly damaged to be recovered after returning from this raid. Flt Lt Tariq Habib was flying this Sabre—the one recorded on Cooke's film. If the report is to be believed, Cooke had two kills that day.

Unfortunately for Cooke, the Hunter he flew that day was loaded with ball ammunition rather than high explosive ammunition. HE ammunition would have set the enemy aircraft on fire. This probably saved the third Sabre from going down because it was the recipient of just a short burst or two of ball ammunition, which would have merely pierced the metal fabric of the aircraft.

In the annals of air combat, Cooke's battle ranks as a classic.

Later, in its official history, the PAF would claim that nine Hunters took on the four Sabres, while in reality, there were only two. The PAF history is a backhanded compliment to the Indian pilots. Cooke went later on to say, 'Wow! What a compliment! Thanks very much—did it feel that there were nine Hunters in the sky?'

The next day, the police recovered the remains of Flt Lt Afzal Khan and the authorities gave him a proper burial at the Muslim cemetery at Kalaikunda.

A few days after this memorable battle, Wing Commander Lafontaine gave orders for the recovery of the Pakistan jet with Pak markings. Unfortunately, the wreckage was not there!

Afzal Khan's Sabre had crashed close to the IIT campus. IIT students sallied forth and made away with parts of the wreckage, whisking them away into the students' hostel. The IAF military police had to raid the students' hostel rooms to recover the wreckage.

Alfred Cooke's Hunter on an emergency landing, cutting in before a PanAm Boeing on long finals. Cooke's Hunter was completely out of fuel

Combat above Kharagpur

2

At the Gates of Lahore

'Battles are won or lost in the mind, before they are won or lost on the ground.'

—Brigadier Desmond Hayde, MVC

In the late afternoon haze of 6 September 1965, the Pakistani village of Dograi was just a blur on the horizon. Looking through his binoculars, Lieutenant Colonel Desmond Hayde, Commanding Officer 3 Jat, could see Pakistani soldiers strengthening their defences and camouflaging their bunkers in and around the village. The scene seemed quiet and peaceful. A sudden glint of light from among the bushes made him focus his binoculars on that spot and he saw what seemed like an officer looking his way. He was sitting on top of a camouflaged bunker and was searching the area in front of him with his binoculars. Lt Col Hayde wondered whether this could be his opposite number tasked with the defence of Dograi. If so, then he would be the Commanding Officer of 3 Baluch.

The Brigade Intelligence Officer had informed him that the enemy battalion holding Dograi was the 3rd Battalion of the Baluch Regiment. The Baluchis were formidable fighters and he wondered what part his battalion would play in the capture of Dograi, which was a task given to his brigade. He knew that if he had to capture Dograi, he would need to use all his military skills to defeat the enemy he was facing.

Looking once again through his binoculars, Lt Col Hayde noticed that the majority of the loopholes of the bunkers faced in his direction. This set him thinking and he decided that if he was given the task to capture Dograi, it would be better to approach it from a direction that his enemy would least expect. He remembered how during World War II, the Germans made the colossal defences of the Maginot Line redundant by turning its defences and attacking from behind. He wondered whether he could do something like that!

The Indian Army had crossed all along the international border in Punjab at 0400 hours on 6 September 1965. Utter secrecy was maintained, to such an extent that even leave parties had not been recalled. 3 Jat was part of 54 Infantry Brigade of 15 Infantry Division and it had arrived at this forward location on the morning of 6 September itself. Normally, troops move from their peace locations to a concentration area in depth, reorganize and move from there to an assembly area and forming-up place (FUP) and then are launched into attack. This time, for reasons of security and to save time, the divisions moved directly from their peace locations to the launching pad and that is how they arrived here that very morning. The Pakistanis were taken by surprise, and the Indian infantry divisions were able to cross the international border and move close to their objectives without much opposition.

The reason for opening the second front in Punjab was that Pakistan's 12 Infantry Division, supported by an armoured brigade and the whole of the Corps artillery, had broken through the defences at Chhamb in the Jammu Sector of J & K and were a few miles from Akhnur. If Akhnur was captured, then the road between Jammu and Poonch would be cut off and the alternative approach to the Valley via the Pir Panjal range would be lost. This adverse situation required a hard decision and the Indian Prime Minister, Lal Bahadur Shastri, took it, opening a second front in Punjab. This would force the Pakistanis to withdraw the bulk of its armour and artillery from the Akhnur front to meet the new threat in Punjab. This is exactly what happened and that is how they were now here sitting close to the Ichhogil Canal.

President Ayub Khan, the President and Head of the armed forces of Pakistan, did not expect India to extend the war from J & K to Punjab. He raved and ranted that this was unfair. According to him, it was all right for Pakistan to attack India in J & K but not all right for India to attack Pakistan in Punjab!

He should have known better, because Prime Minister Lal Bahadur Shastri had warned Pakistan on 28 April 1965 that an attack on Jammu and Kashmir would be considered an attack on India and he would take decisions in the best interest of his country. This implied that India would respond at a time and place of its own choosing. Ayub Khan, however, did not seem to have got that message.

The opening of the second front in Punjab entailed offensives by the Indian Army's XI Corps and I Corps. As part of the overall plan of Headquarters XI Corps, three infantry divisions were tasked to advance towards Lahore. This story concerns 3 Jat and 54 Infantry Brigade, which were part of 15 Infantry Division. 54 Infantry Brigade commanded by Brigadier M.S. Rikh was ordered to push forward to the line of the Ichhogil Canal, capture Dograi, move forward as part of the Division and threaten Lahore. 3 Jat at that time was in reserve for the capture of Dograi.

Notwithstanding the fact that opening a second front in Punjab was strategically a great decision, the fact was that the formations and units who were tasked to execute the offensive were newly raised and not fully equipped or trained. I Corps, which was a strike corps, and 14 Infantry Division had commenced raising just a few months earlier in April and 6 Mountain Division had not been equipped or trained to fight in the plains. In fact, most of the formations and units were ill-prepared for war in August 1965.

That was the situation at that time, but the Government and the armed forces had no option but to take this call and make the best of a bad situation. Lt Col Desmond Hayde had taken over 3 Jat just a week earlier.

3 Jat had recently arrived from the Eastern sector. As a consequence, they had no recoilless guns (anti-tank guns) because there was no threat from enemy armour in the north-east and no one in the battalion had fired

that weapon in the past four years. Battalion mortars and medium machine guns were new models that the troops were not familiar with and had not been fired on the long ranges, and the battalion was deficient by the equivalent strength of one rifle company.[1]

According to the Commanding Officer (CO), the officers present in 3 Jat at that time were down-to-earth regimental types and not the sort who were highly qualified in various courses that marked them for higher ranks.[2] None had qualified for the Staff College or been graded fit to be instructors at army schools of instruction. But they knew their men had sound knowledge of ground and basic tactics and, most importantly, they had the instinct of the warrior race and were raring to get to grips with the enemy. They were the type of officers on which good regiments are built. They had in their service tenure shared the dangers, discomforts and deprivations with the men. They epitomized regimental spirit at its best—a major battle-winning factor.

The Ichhogil Canal was a brick-lined canal with 45-degree slopes on both sides. The depth of water was 20 feet with a speed of 2 to 3 knots, and the width at the top of the canal was 112 feet—a formidable obstacle by all accounts.

Common military knowledge dictated that 3 Baluch would have a screen position ahead of Dograi and the importance of Dograi would demand that the strength of this screen would be an infantry company. The most likely location of the screen would be at Dial village. This was confirmed by fighting patrols from 3 Jat.

Although 3 Jat was to be in reserve for the capture of Dograi, the responsibility for this capture ultimately fell upon this battalion. The CO decided to first eliminate the enemy screen position at Dial before tackling the main defence position at Dograi.

Screen positions are only meant to give warning to the main defensive position about the strength and direction of an enemy attack, to delay the enemy if possible and to get back to the battalion's defensive position to fight the main defensive battle. The Commanding Officer 3 Jat decided to destroy the screen position at Dial village itself, so that its personnel would not be able to take part in the battle for Dograi. Since this would be the first operation for the battalion after many years, the CO decided to use maximum strength for elimination of the enemy's screen position.

The force ratio for the capture of an enemy position is 3:1, i.e., the force that is attacking needs to be three times the force that is defending, because the attacking force gets diminished because of casualties due to enemy mines, artillery, MMG (medium machine guns) and tank fire. So, by the time the attacking force reaches the enemy position, its strength should be at least equal to the strength of the defender. Therefore, the force to be used to assault and capture Dograi should have been a force equivalent to that of a brigade. It was decided, however, that 3 Jat would take on this task of a battalion versus a battalion, because the forces available did not allow a larger force to be used. Unconventional, but that is how it was, and most importantly, the CO 3 Jat felt that he could do it.

The attack on the screen position was carried out on 6 September without the benefit of prior reconnaissance, knowledge of ground or elementary intelligence concerning enemy strength and dispositions, and is a unique example of pure battlefield instinct. The screen was overrun by tackling it from the rear. A sharp fight followed and forty-eight of the enemy were accounted for in dead, wounded and captured, but 3 Jat also suffered five killed and ten wounded. The success of this operation was achieved without the support of own artillery fire or that of battalion support weapons. Not using artillery fire or battalion support weapons added to the surprise factor and so the Baluchis was stunned to suddenly find 3 Jat behind them. They tried to turn their defences around but it was too late.

After the enemy screen position was eliminated, the battalion dug in and consolidated its position. They managed to do this just in time because the PAF attacked and strafed their position at 0630 hours on the morning of 7 September. By 0830 hours, the battalion had been strafed three times. The Brigade Headquarters also suffered casualties from the strafing.

The subsequent advance to the Ichhogil Canal was carried out under heavy enemy artillery shelling and successive air strikes and is an example of boldness, initiative and exploitation by 3 Jat at its best. The extent of the enemy defences as they became visible, coupled with the intensity of ground fire, would have justified that the attack on Dograi be taken by a brigade. At the height of this baptism of fire, as the bodies of the soldiers of 3 Jat hurtled through the air or crumpled into heaps, the battalion got news that most of its F Echelon vehicles had been lost in an air strike. Still, the Jats carried on with their advance resolutely because the CO knew that it would be best to attack Dograi soonest, before the Pakistanis could reinforce the position with armour and infantry.

The battalion moved up for the capture of Dograi along with a troop of armour. The CO had already decided that he would take Dograi from the rear and he swung his battalion towards the north of Dograi with 'D' Company and a troop of armour in the lead followed by the CO's party and the remaining companies. The rest of the squadron of armour was held in the rear to be used on either flank as the battle progressed.

The battalion was able to move out of range of the small arms fire from Dograi but was plastered effectively by accurate enemy artillery fire. Pakistani forward artillery observers brought effective fire on anything that moved.

They were bold and held on to their observation posts to the last man. Pakistani recce and support units mounted on jeeps with recoilless anti-tank guns (RCL) and MMGs ranged widely, probing gaps and firing at anything they saw. This made the movement of 3 Jat very difficult.

The PAF launched successful air strikes on the assaulting Indian units and formations. Brigadier M.S. Rikh, the Brigade Commander, was severely wounded and had to be evacuated. A new commander had to be found and Brigadier S.S. Kalha, Commander of the Corps Artillery Brigade, was detailed to fill the gap and he took command of the brigade. Indian soldiers kept looking at the sky for the Indian fighter aircraft to take on the PAF, but the Indian Air Force was conspicuous by its absence.

The IAF was focusing on its interdiction role rather than supporting the troops on the ground.

After a sharp fight with the enemy defences approximately 1200 yards north of Dograi, 'D' Company secured the first lodgement on the east bank of the Ichhogil Canal. This turned the enemy defences of Dograi completely and the Baluchis were now facing the wrong way. They decided to abandon their defences and Dograi was entered and cleared by 3 Jat, and the troop of armour in support was signalled to come forward.

The enemy continued to fire from high ground further west where the Bata Shoe Factory was located. This factory overlooked Dograi and was not shown on Indian maps. It became evident that it would be impossible to hold Dograi without neutralizing the dominating heights of Batapore. Lt Col Hayde decided to exploit on towards Batapore. Even before its armour could come up, 3 Jat moved forward to capture Batapore. 'A' Company was ordered to advance to Attoke Awan as a preliminary before putting 'C' Company into Batapore.

'A' Company was halfway to Attoke Awan when enemy armour made its appearance. This was a dangerous situation but the Jats had been taught that in such situations, it was best to disperse and 'go to ground' as tanks would find it difficult to deal with infantry who had taken position at ground level. Initially, some of the soldiers must have been petrified because of the exposure to the new danger of these huge tanks, but they soon overcame this fear through their resolve and an understanding that this danger too could be overcome.

The Battle of Dograi: PAF Sabre jets attacking Indian infantry

The Jats fought back against enemy armour with small arms and the comforting cover of the ground and the headstones in a cemetery. The armour for some unknown reason pulled back and a major disaster was avoided. After a while, enemy armour made another foray against the Jats but by this time, our own tanks of 14 Horse had fetched up and two enemy tanks were quickly destroyed. The Pakistani armour once again withdrew. 'C' Company 3 Jat now occupied the major portion of the Batapore Shoe Factory and the rest of the battalion sat astride the Ichhogil Canal–GT Road crossing, supported by just one troop (three tanks) of 14 Horse. The sub-units to provide signal communication and the artillery observation parties had not fetched up nor had any of the commanders or other troops, so the brigade was unaware of the situation at Dograi–Batapore. 3 Jat were now in a dominating position and, had the rest of the brigade built up on the battalion, they would have been in a comfortable position to take on whatever the Pakistanis could throw at them. Batapore Shoe Factory was just about 12 miles from Lahore and the aim of 'threatening' Lahore would have been achieved.

Except for a few hours respite, taken the previous day at the start of the attack, the men of 3 Jat had had no rest. They had suffered continuous shelling, air strikes, machine gun and small arms fire for most of the day and had eleven killed and forty-four wounded. The battalion took a battering from enemy armour, artillery and the PAF. In the words of the Lt Col Hayde:

> Enemy artillery turned the area held by the Jats into a shroud of grey mist, the PAF searched the ground for the men of 3 Jat raking the length of the battalion with rockets and cannons. Into this would penetrate the unmistakable roar of enemy tanks closing for what they supposed was a kill. The Battalion could well have been annihilated.

The battalion survived because every man fought back. The CO, a company commander and many others got wounded and the battalion's Intelligence Officer (IO) was killed. The battalion's single RCL got knocked out by enemy tank fire but the Jats, undaunted, fired at the enemy armour with their rocket launchers, 2-inch and 81 mm mortars and MMGs. There was defiance amongst the men and a strong resolve not to let the enemy get the better of them. The last enemy armour assault came at 1630 hours, but the enemy infantry assault that was expected to follow failed to materialize and the Jats now knew that they had carried the day.

The brigade, however, could not build up on the defence line set up by the Jats. Failure of the rest of the brigade to join them made their situation untenable. It was extremely disappointing that they had to be called back. The Jats were angry. They took this as an insult not only to the *izzat* of the regiment but also a failure to appreciate and take advantage of their hard-won results and the sacrifices that had been made to capture Dograi and advance to Batapore. To be called back when they had reached the 'Gates of Lahore' was frustrating to say the least.

At this stage of the battle, on 8 September, Dograi was vacant and it could have been occupied by the brigade. However, the other two battalions of the brigade were recovering from the outcomes of their own battles and were not in a position to occupy and hold Dograi. After the Jats had returned to base, a conversation between CO 3 Jat and the Brigade Commander at midday on 10 September went something like this:

Brigade Commander (Bde Cdr): 'Well, that's that. What do we do now? I've still got orders to get up to the Ichhogil Canal line.'

CO 3 Jat (CO): 'If you want Dograi, I can give it to you tonight; or tomorrow for that matter.'

Bde Cdr: 'Alone?'

CO: 'Yes, alone—but we don't want it to be like last time, get there and then be called back.'

Bde Cdr: 'The other two battalions have to be given time to settle down. Let's hold on for a few days.'[3]

Pakistan's 10 and 11 Infantry Divisions were responsible for the defence of Lahore. Whereas 10 Pakistani Infantry Division would occupy defence positions forward of Lahore, 11 Pakistani Infantry Division was charged with carrying out offensive operations forward of Lahore to ensure its security or would combine with an armoured division as part of a strike corps to carry out offensive operations against India.

The situation now developed where India needed to capture Dograi once again in order to threaten Lahore, and Pakistan needed to re-occupy Dograi to ensure Lahore's security. Whereas Pakistan had resources of infantry and armour to re-occupy Dograi, India's 54 Infantry brigade had only 3 Jat to recapture it.

Major General Sarfraz Khan, GOC Pakistan 10 Infantry Division tasked Brigadier Abdul Qayyum Sher, Commander 22 Pakistan Infantry Brigade, to occupy Dograi on the night of 7/8 September along with 23 Cav and companies of 18 Baluch and 15 Frontier Force.

Two days passed before the 54 Indian Infantry Brigade was in a position to occupy Dograi, but by this time, Pakistan had re-occupied Dograi with the forces mentioned above and more. Dograi would now be a hard nut to crack. On 12 September, Brigadier S.S. Kalha told Lt Col Hayde, 'Okay! You attack Dograi on the night of 14/15. Let me know what help you need.'

Lt Col Hayde had earlier stated that if Dograi had to be captured, he would do it alone, but the force holding Dograi had now multiplied. His decision to do it alone was based on the honour of the Jats, but he now wondered whether he had bitten off more than he could chew. In view of his going alone, he decided that the plan had to be simple and that it would devolve on three simple factors: the order in which the rifle companies would attack, the direction of the attack and the timing of the attack. He had in his mind a clear picture of the geography of the village after his battalion had captured it the first time. He reduced Dograi to four extremities or corners and so he divided the objective into four parts. And he had four rifle companies—one part of Dograi to each rifle company! He decided that there was no need to go through a lengthy 'appreciation of the situation', which is how it was normally done and to get his plan approved by brigade and division—there was no time for that! He knew that the weakest part of the enemy defences of Dograi was the north-eastern part of the village and decided that this should be his entry point to Dograi. This would be the door that would have to be opened to allow the companies to enter Dograi and go for their objectives.

The open spaces to the north of this part of his objective would enable a night move and the noise of water flowing in a canal distributary would help his troops to maintain direction at night. Also, all four parts of Dograi had to be captured well before first light to avoid interference by the PAF the next morning. He decided to work backwards from dawn to calculate the time to move and approach Dograi, and enough time for each of his companies to secure their part of their objective without getting in each other's way.

This brought him to fix the time to launch his attack at 2230 hours on 15 September 1965.

Brigadier Niranjan Singh Kullar, MC, had in the meanwhile, been posted in and assumed command of 54 Infantry Brigade at around 1600 hours, 12 September, and Brigadier S.S. Kalha reverted to his appointment as Commander Corps Artillery Brigade. The new Brigade Commander's first action was to cancel the Jat attack on Dograi because he wanted to ensure that the plan had every chance of success and that necessary support was available. His second action was to tell the Jats that the attack had not been cancelled—it had only been postponed.

The H-Hour for the attack was postponed to 0230 hours of 17 September.

Lt Col Hayde knew just how Dograi had to be captured and each and every man had been briefed on the role that he would have to play in this epic battle. He made sure that his troops were not kept idle in the intervening period of 12 to 17 September. For all ranks of 3 Jat, he made sure that it was a period of physical and mental preparation that would climax at the moment when the attack would go in. He dominated the area between him and the enemy by strong fighting patrols. Familiarization with the intervening ground and objectives was achieved. They had experienced Pakistani fire power and fighting capabilities at first hand and knew it was something that could be dealt with. He spoke to his officers, JCOs and senior NCOs. He said, 'The aim of patrolling is to dominate the enemy. We will go out into no-man's-land[4] tonight and every night. By the time we attack Dograi again, there should be not a single inch of ground between us that is not known.' Patrolling and preliminary operations produced total domination over the enemy.

These patrols jittered[5] the defenders of Dograi by closing up to their defences and making them respond to their fire. By this, they were able to locate the enemy medium machine guns, light machine guns and other weapons. The Pakistanis ought to have been sending out their patrols to prevent 3 Jat from getting to know the lie of the land and the organization of their defences, but they were busy fortifying their defences. Only later did they think of sending out their own patrols, but by then the Jat patrols were already at their doorstep. These actions revealed the differences between the Pakistani and the Indian infantry. While the infantry of the Indian Army believed in the infantry soldier getting close to the enemy by exploiting tactical use of ground and small arms, the Pakistan Army believed in using heavy and concentrated use of fire to discourage domination of the intervening ground by the enemy and their infantry was thus relegated to a supporting role.

The Pakistanis reacted to the activities of the Jat patrols by firing Verey lights[6] and parachute flares that lit up the night sky. Streams of tracer-lit medium machine gun bullets erupted from all along the line of the Pakistani defences and down came their artillery DFs.[7] All this frightened the Pakistanis themselves. It was their own mine-laying and wire-laying parties who invariably rushed back to their defences to avoid being shot in the back and being sandwiched between the fire of our patrols and their own defensive fire. For the Jats, it emboldened them and increased their confidence; they were able to pinpoint the automatic weapons being used by the enemy and the location of the artillery DF tasks.[15]

The attack plan that sent all the rifle companies of the battalion in the assault in a single phase is possibly unprecedented. It is more than likely that no battalion has been ever launched with the rifle companies attacking the objective from different directions in a single phase.

The final orders given to the troops were so simple that every soldier knew exactly what he had to do, when and how he had to do it. Such orders will not be found in any training manual or aide-memoire. Soldiers were told to follow their section commanders, sections the platoon commanders and platoon commanders their company commanders who 'will lead you straight to your objective. On securing your objective, make your firing position immediately. Thereafter DO NOT MOVE and shoot at anything that moves,' went the words of Lt Col Hayde.

Whereas the new Brigade Commander was aggressive and in total agreement with the course of action suggested by Lt Col Hayde, the Division Commander, however, was sceptical about 3 Jat being able to capture Dograi on its own.

Part of a conversation between the Brigade Commander and the Division Commander ran something like this:

Cdr 54 Bde: 'If you want to do something why don't you let the Jats take Dograi?'

GOC: 'Come on, how they can take Dograi on their own?'

Cdr 54 Bde: 'The CO told me the very day I arrived that 3 Jat was ready to take Dograi again, at any time, day or night.'

GOC: 'Do you believe that? Can the Jats actually capture Dograi on their own?'

Cdr 54 Bde: 'I believe they can. Not only because the CO says so but also because I've spoken to the men and they believe that the capture of Dograi is part of their destiny.'[8]

There are very few instances where a unit is given an option to give up an attack, especially one such as this, loaded as it was, with the possibility of a total wipe-out, and to insist on carrying it out, despite all the imponderables, and that too doing it on its own.

Lt Col Hayde decided to address his troops and fire them up for the impending assault on Dograi. He knew that during war, soldiers need to know the position exactly as it is. No whitewashing or bluffing will work. He spoke to the Jats in their native Haryanvi. He called upon the traditional honour of the Jats who considered themselves the best fighters in the world. He told them that they had captured Dograi once and pulling them back was a slur on their honour. Dograi was theirs and only theirs to capture once again and the honour to capture Dograi could not be given to any other unit. He made no bones about the fact that it would be a tough fight because Dograi had been reinforced, that many would die and many more would be wounded, but this was a small price to pay for the honour of the Jats, the Jat regiment and the honour of India. He added, that if he, as their Commanding Officer, was killed in the fighting, he wanted his body to be carried into Dograi because that is where he wanted to be the following morning when Dograi was captured. Then he shouted: 'Where will we be tomorrow morning?' And the battalion roared: 'In Dograi.' The roar from the men reverberated across the Ichhogil Canal and the Pakistanis surely heard it. They must have wondered what the Jats were up to and got apprehensive as to what was going to happen next.

The brigade finalized 21 September as the date for the attack and the H-Hour for the phase of the attack by 3 Jat would be 0130 hours. Postponing the H-Hour reduced the time for the Jats to capture their objectives if Dograi had to be in their hands before first light. Feint attacks were launched on the nights of 18/19 and 19/20 September with strong patrols simulating a charge. Those nights exploded into sound and light shows, with the enemy reacting vigorously to the deception attacks. The aim was to confuse the enemy so that on the night of the actual attack, the enemy would think this was just one of those attacks where nothing really happens. The real objective was kept out of these deception attacks so that the Baluchis would be kept in the dark. It was important for the Jats that the first assault by 'D' Company was a success, as it would open the door for the remaining companies to enter Dograi one after another.

Fired up by the CO's address, every soldier of 3 Jat knew that many would die that night, but they told themselves, 'We are the Jats, the leading warrior race of history. We will not let the CO or the *kaum* or the Regiment down.' They told each other, 'If I am wounded, carry me forward and put me down on the objective.' The soldiers of 3 Jat no longer suffered from the valour of ignorance. They knew what was expected of them and what they would do.[9]

While the Jats were waiting for their H-Hour so that they could move forward, the CO received a message on the wireless from the Brigade Commander that Phase 1 of the attack was not successful:

Bde Cdr: 'Sorry to say, Phase 1 has not taken off. What do you want to do?'

CO 3 Jat: 'We carry on.'

Bde Cdr: 'Why not postpone it—for a day or two?'

CO 3 Jat: 'We do it now, regardless, or not at all. We opt for now. In fact, we are at it already.'

Bde Cdr: 'I am repeating the fire plan for twenty minutes, adjust accordingly and good luck.'

Artillery to cover the move of 3 Jat commenced and at the same time, a neighbouring brigade began attacking to the north of Dograi, so there was plenty of noise to cover 3 Jat. 'D' Company was followed by the CO's party, 'C' Company, 'B' Company, 'A' Company and Battalion HQ. Each company's move was staggered time-wise so that they would not tangle with each other. They moved silently like ghosts. After a while, the CO came upon 'D' Company, which had stopped. On asking why, the Company Commander replied that it appeared that the enemy had pulled out from their defences into the stronger buildings behind. Meanwhile, 'D' Company raced towards their objective—the north-eastern edge of Dograi. The enemy now realized that this was the real thing and there erupted withering fire from every conceivable weapon.

It was an unbelievable sight! Imagine a night brilliantly lit by exploding shells, parachute flares, Verey lights and tracer bullets. 'D' Company had just jarred the door open to Dograi; 'C' Company was streaming by on the right with 'B' Company doing the same on the left and the CO's party was sandwiched somewhere in between. These three companies had to immediately and almost simultaneously secure firm footholds on their objectives. No sooner had 'C' Company gained access to the Dograi buildings than an unknown and unexpected enemy position surfaced, erupting with a withering blast from no less than eight heavy and light automatics spaced over a mere 200 yards, giving the appearance of a wall of fire. It appeared that this outburst would put an end to the Jat assault.

However, 3 Jat seemed to have a man for every occasion. This time it was Subedar Pale Ram, MM (Military Medal) and thrice Mentioned-in-Dispatches in earlier wars. Rising above the incredible din of the battle and taking complete control of the situation, he shouted, *'Sab jawan dahine taraf mere saath* CHARGE.' It was an awesome sight, a supreme honour for anyone who witnessed it: Subedar Pale Ram's unequivocal charge leading 108 men. The right hand and depth platoons of 'C' Company and the depth platoon of 'D' Company turned without hesitation into the charge. What was left of the CO's party could only look on in wonder at the lines of Jats blotting out the wall of fire.

It must rank among one of the finest infantry charges and the noblest acts of gallantry of all time, deserving of the highest award. Into that wall of fire and death raced Pale Ram and 108 men. Pale Ram took six bullets in his chest and stomach, yet his body was found on top of an enemy bunker. It is difficult to believe how he carried those bullets along in his fabulous charge. Out of this glorious onslaught emerged only twenty-seven of the unbelievably brave 108.

The remaining platoons of 'C' Company fell on the remaining trenches and bunkers and the third platoon of 'D' Company rushed past and attacked the trenches further north. 'B' Company emerged on GT Road, found the enemy facing the wrong way and made short work of them. 'A' Company, led by Major Tyagi, rushed towards their objective. In his headlong charge, he received a bullet in his chest, yet he staggered on until he was struck down once again amongst the enemy tanks. His last cry was, '*Tanko ko pehle marna, Jat Balwan.*' 'A' Company responded to their Company Commander's last wish—two enemy tanks were knocked out with their rocket launchers (RLs) and the remaining enemy armour withdrew. There was bitter fighting on the objective but by first light, Dograi was in the hands of the Jats. Enemy artillery commenced heavy shelling and no one could see Dograi because of the dust and smoke. The PAF was guided by the smoke and dust and repeatedly strafed the

Jats. Brigadier Niranjan Singh came up on the wireless and asked Lt Col Hayde, 'Are you all right?'

Wounded soldiers who could have easily been evacuated preferred instead to remain and be treated on the battlefield, and the regimental medical officer (RMO), Captain Timmaareddi, was more than equal to the job. Most outstanding in this respect was Subedar Khazan Singh, VrC. Receiving a head wound in the very first action on 6 September, which left pieces of lead implanted in his head and wounded yet again on 21 September during the preliminary recce for the final attack, he went to hospital only after the ceasefire.

A Pakistani counter-attack to recapture Dograi ran into the neighbouring 38 Indian Infantry Brigade. Another battle was fought on the sidelines of Dograi, but the Pakistani counter-attack petered out and they retired from where they had come. The Jats now commenced mopping up operations. Khaki-clad corpses[10] littered the area and a body count of the Pakistani dead was undertaken. The Brigade Commander got an engineering company to collect the Pakistani war dead from the gullies, lanes and courtyards of Dograi. The total dead came to a near unbelievable 900, and these did not account for those who fell into the canal and were swept away. Pakistani officers and soldiers now began to surrender. The prisoners grew to such numbers that they became difficult to handle. They were marched off to the rear under the custody of the Naib Subedar Adjutant. They included five officers and 104 other ranks. Unknown to 3 Jat, Dograi had been reinforced by elements of a number of Pakistani infantry, artillery and armoured units. Prisoners listed by the

Brigade Major of 54 Indian Infantry Brigade included CO 16 Punjab, his battery commander, two more officers and others. The dead and the prisoners belonged to 8 Punjab, 12 Punjab, 16 Punjab (major contribution), 3 Baluch, 18 Baluch, 13 TDU[11], 23 Cavalry, artillery and recce and support elements.

Jat casualties were loaded on a T-16 Carrier[12] and ferried rearwards through mine fields, and tank and artillery fire. One of the first to be evacuated was Subedar Pale Ram. Almost as incredible as the charge he led, is that he survived! This incredible individual was recovering from his wounds in the hospital when the hospital ward MO came across him putting on his uniform and getting ready to leave the hospital. When the doctor asked him what he was doing and where he was intending to go, he answered, 'I must get back to my battalion. I have heard that Pakistan has restarted the war!'

It came to be known that the enemy was in much greater strength than the attackers believed, as was seen when the body count was done. The disadvantage of adverse relative strength appears to have been overcome by the sheer speed of the assault, the surprise gained at the point of impact and tackling the enemy from the rear, thereby destroying their depth defences and reserves that led to the collapse of the Pakistani companies, not to forget the high spirits of the soldiers of 3 Jat.

Meanwhile, the UN was pushing for a ceasefire. When it finally came into effect, the exhausted Jat soldiers—officers and men—fell into a deep sleep. They had been fighting non-stop for over thirty-six hours. Only Captain Timmaareddi, the RMO, was awake, as he continued to dress the wounds of the sleeping Jat soldiers. Visitors, in the form of senior commanders, came over to congratulate the Jats on their brilliant victory but they were fast asleep. Some of them, in their sleep, did manage to offer a soft 'Ram Ram' to the passing visitors.

Postscript: The 'D' Factor

The epic success of 3 Jat in the operations of 1965 is attributed to the powerful presence of the 'D' Factor. What is this factor?

In the words of Brigadier Hayde, it is that compound that develops from the military way of life. When that way is lived, especially by the officers, it becomes the catalyst for the highest levels of conduct. In this, danger, deprivation and discomfort are shared by all ranks as are the joy, pride and high spirits when challenges spring up, are met and conquered with great decisiveness. In this, the officers are seen 'to lead', the JCOs 'to push' and the men 'to perform'.

The 'D' Factor does not arrive overnight. It builds up from year to year, through the process of command and being commanded in every sphere and every aspect of life in the unit. Bright new brooms try sometimes to sweep clean, but it is the old, sturdy, well-known, used and properly maintained broom that does the job. There is pride in executing every job, large or small, that becomes the driving force at every level.

A battalion does not have to be exceptionally brilliant to perform well—just sound basics are enough. All that the soldier needs to do is remember and perform the drills that he has been taught and arduously practised, time and again, until it becomes second nature to him and challenges are met and dealt with effectively. That is why 3 Jat opted for and was capable of achieving what it did. The plans and objectives of the 'higher command' were met by an empowered battalion, confident of its ability to deliver, irrespective of the obstacles that would come its way. All that the higher command did was to place the right unit in the right place and allow it to do what it said it would do. Events on the battlefield were thereafter dealt with and disposed of in a competent manner and exploited by keen and vigilant commanders.

All power to the 'D' Factor!

Introspection

Was the Battle of Dograi worth it?

By 17 September, the reputation of 3 Jat stood very high. The CO was already highly decorated with more to come for others. The battalion did not need to do anything more to prove itself. Besides, the Lahore front had stabilized along the line of contact, which did not appear to be in any danger of getting jolted.

Yet, 3 Jat attacked Dograi again, displaying all the time that there was a compulsion to do so, regardless that it would cost heavily in casualties, which, in fact, it did—216. Was it really worth it?

There lurks at the back of the mind of every true soldier, the spirit of honour that something still remains to be done so that the name of their family, race and the regiment to which they belong will forever be remembered with honour.

Dograi stood out as a challenge. At no other place was the enemy so numerous and compactly located. Its defences and firepower were formidable. The place's name was already famous; a prize such as only fleetingly appears on the battlefield. Such a challenge, at whatever the risk, was too compelling to be denied.

3 Jat was lucky to be in that stage of interplay between officers, JCOs and men, which had created tremendous feelings of loyalty and confidence, demanding from each man the highest measure of fidelity and courage.

The battle of Dograi has brought honour to both the living and the dead of those who took part, and to the Jat race and the Jat Regiment.

It is that which made it worthwhile.

The narrative of this epic battle is mostly in the words of Brigadier Desmond Hayde, MVC. I have only put together his story from his book *The Battle of Dograi*, from a pamphlet with the same name issued by the United Service Institution of India, and from correspondence and dialogue with the Brigadier many years ago.

In his own words, he mentioned that the plan conceived by him for the attack on the night of 21/22 September would undoubtedly have earned him the assessment of being 'unfit for command' had he propounded it at a training exercise or on a course of instruction. Relative strength, the size of the objective and its strong build-up would have precluded the thought of putting up an attack of this dimension. And yet, it succeeded!

It was necessary that after Dograi was captured it had to be held by at least a brigade to allow for strong counter-attacks from the Pakistani defenders. Lahore was just 12 miles away and the reaction was bound to be violent.

This battle absolutely establishes regimental spirit as a battle-winning factor. I hope those in high places—civil and military—are listening!

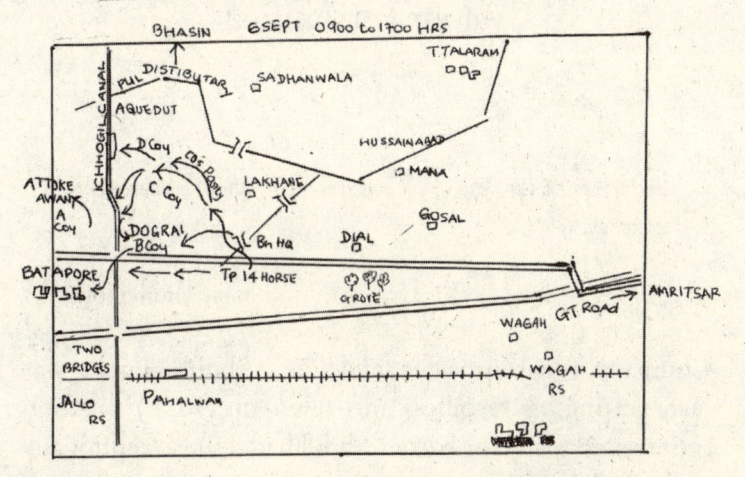

The battle of Dograi (USI pamphlet, Map 3)

3

Valour Personified

'Achievers never expose themselves, but their achievements expose them.'

—Anonymous

Company Quartermaster Havildar[1] Abdul Hamid was busy getting his recoilless anti-tank gun (RCL)[2] platoon trained and ready for battle. Abdul had done exceptionally well on the RCL course and the Commanding Officer, Maj. Gen. Farhat Bhatty, VSM, MiD, decided that he would be the best person to take charge and train the RCL detachments because he knew that Punjab was armour country and his RCL guns would play a decisive role in a future infantry-tank battle. He could not imagine, at that moment, how true was his assessment and how good was his choice in selecting Abdul Hamid as his RCL platoon commander!

The battalion had been tasked to move to the Shuga Sector (Uttarakhand) to take over defences on the Sino-Indian border. The advance party, consisting of his second-in-command, company and specialist platoon commanders, had already moved when fresh orders were received that his unit would now be deployed for operations in Punjab. Lt Col Bhatty was doing his best to reorganize the command and control of his battalion so that the most proficient persons assumed leadership roles in all the right places. He was left with very young officers but what they lacked in experience, they more than made up in their eagerness to deliver the best results. His strength was in the JCOs and senior NCOs, his second tier of junior leaders, who had loads of experience and more than made up for the absence of his first tier of leaders.

The opening of a second front in Punjab during the 1965 war was a bold decision by India's Prime Minister Shri Lal Bahadur Shastri, to draw Pakistani forces away from the Chhamb-Jaurian Sector and also entice them into the plains of Punjab and Sialkot, with a view to destroy them in infantry-tank battles.

In order to maintain surprise, 4, 7 and 15 Infantry Divisions of India's XI Corps advanced directly from their peace locations to their assembly areas on the night of 5/6 September 1965 and crossed the international border before dawn on 6 September. Complete surprise was achieved, resulting in a series of successes in the initial phase of this operation.

XI Corps was given the task of securing the line of the Ichhogil Canal, establishing bridgeheads across the canal and thereafter threatening Lahore. 4 Indian Infantry Division, after advancing some distance across the international border, took up defensive positions to consolidate the areas captured. It was expected that

Pakistan forces would react violently and provide XI Corps the opportunity to destroy them. After initially being taken by surprise, Pakistan got their act together to launch their contingency plans to thwart India's offensive.

Pakistan's 'Strike Corps' consisting of the 1st Armoured Division and 11 Infantry Division concentrated at Kasur to launch a major counter-offensive into India. Unknown to XI Corps, 4 Indian Infantry Division had broken into the axis of ingress of Pakistan's 1st Armoured Division, and 4 Grenadiers happened to be bang in the middle of the path of the Pakistani armoured division. This resulted in a form of 'spoiling attack' which delayed the advance of the Pakistani offensive forces in this sector.

It was decided that Asal Uttar would be a suitable place to counter Pakistan's offensive, rather than Khem Karan, which could be bypassed. Asal Uttar covered both the Khem Karan–Amritsar axis as well as the Khem Karan–Patti axis. The Pakistani armoured brigade attacked exactly as anticipated on 10 September 1965 and attempted to break through. It attempted to overrun the 4 Grenadiers position, but the battalion held out with great determination and gallantry against the heavy pressure exerted upon them.

4 Grenadiers, which had arrived at midnight from the area of the Ichhogil Canal, commenced to dig down. By the morning of 8 September, the trenches had gone down barely 3 feet. No overhead cover was possible and no camouflage was necessary as the battalion was in the midst of thick sugarcane fields.

4 Grenadiers is a unique example of a battalion that distinguished itself in an intensely fought war without

its regular company and specialist platoon commanders. Very junior company officers and senior JCOs were consequently elevated to fight this battle.

CQMH Abdul Hamid was directed to take on the role of the anti-tank detachment commander. The battalion had handed over its RCL guns and on receiving the warning order to move to Punjab, CQMH Abdul Hamid was sent to the Ordnance depot to get new RCL guns. Abdul Hamid had just enough time to collect the guns, to zero[3] them and get them ready for battle. He had done well at the RCL course at Infantry School, Mhow, and that is how a CQMH came to be in charge of a detachment of RCL guns.

At 0730 hours, 8 September, the rumbling sound of a large number of enemy tanks was heard and at 0900 hours, a troop of Patton tanks came astride the road heading in the direction of 4 Grenadiers. Abdul Hamid held his fire and when the leading tank was barely 30 yards away, he fired his RCL gun and knocked it out. The tank caught fire and the crew of the two follow-up tanks abandoned their armoured vehicles and fled.

At 1130 hours came a second attack by another troop of Pattons preceded by heavy artillery shelling. Abdul Hamid knocked out yet another tank, his second, and again the crew of the two follow-up tanks abandoned their tanks and fled. At the end of the day of 8 September, Abdul had destroyed two enemy tanks and in addition, four of them, in running condition, lay abandoned on the battlefield.

In response to a frantic demand for mines by 4 Grenadiers, an engineer company came forward and laid anti-tank and anti-personnel mines.

Puzzled at the destruction of its tanks, the Pakistan armoured division asked for an air strike on the Indian defences. At 0900 hours on 9 September, the Grenadiers' defence position was attacked by four Sabre jets without causing any damage. The air attack was followed by three more armour assaults at 0930, 1130 and 1430 hours. Abdul Hamid destroyed two more enemy tanks and some anti-tank mines were heard exploding. By the evening of 9 September, Abdul Hamid had destroyed four Pattons. By this time the battalion had accounted for thirteen Patton tanks and some more lay abandoned in the minefield.

It was clear by then that the battalion was facing a concentrated armour assault by an enemy armoured brigade. Surprisingly, the enemy armour assaults were not accompanied by infantry attacks.

A squadron of Indian Shermans was withdrawn from the battlefield as their shells were ineffective against the armour of the Patton tanks. Indian Centurion tanks which had come forward briefly were also withdrawn as they were needed to fight a major tank battle that was about to take place in the Asal Uttar area.

4 Grenadiers was now left alone with its four RCL guns, a hastily scattered minefield and the determination of its men to hold on against overwhelming odds. The morale of the battalion, however, was sky-high. After all, they had accounted for more enemy tanks with just their RCL guns than any unit could ever hope for. Abdul Hamid had, by this time, been recommended for the award of a Param Vir Chakra for his outstanding performance in destroying three enemy Pattons.

On 10 September, the defences of 4 Grenadiers were subjected to heavy shelling by Pakistani artillery. A dawn attack by Pakistani infantry supported by armour was expected but failed to take place. The assault pattern remained the same. It seemed that the Pakistanis were unable to learn any lessons from its failures of the previous two days.

The first assault on 10 September came at 0830 hours by a troop of tanks—one tank on the road and two on the lower verges of the road about 200 yards away. Strict fire control was observed and when the tanks came close enough, Abdul Hamid destroyed one more tank and moved his RCL gun to an alternative fire position. At 0900 hours, the enemy again pressed forward with increased artillery support and Abdul destroyed one more tank—his sixth! This was followed by increased artillery shelling. Due to his open RCL jeep being vulnerable to the heavy enemy artillery shelling, Abdul Hamid told his crew to take cover and he would handle the gun on his own. The next tank and Abdul Hamid spotted each other simultaneously. He needed to shift his position immediately. Being alone, he could not do that and yet engage the enemy tank, so he reloaded the RCL gun and traversed it. But without help to reload the gun and to aim and fire, his reaction was slower than earlier. By this time both Abdul Hamid and the tank gunner had placed each other in the crosshairs of their sights and fired nearly simultaneously. Abdul Hamid was killed instantly. The battalion history states that they both fired simultaneously and blew each other to bits.

By this time the award of the Param Vir Chakra had come through, but Abdul Hamid had been killed. For its courageous conduct against overwhelming odds, the battalion was awarded the battle honour of Asal Uttar and the theatre honour of Punjab.

Not to be forgotten is the dramatic manner in which the commander of the artillery brigade of Pakistan's 1st Armoured Division was killed and the GOC wounded within the battalion-defended area of 4 Grenadiers.

The GOC 1st Armoured Division, Major General Nasir Ahmed, was surveying the battlefield from his helicopter but was unable to fathom why he was unable to break through the Indian defences. Accompanied by his Commander Artillery Brigadier A.R. Shammi and his Recce Group (R Group), he came forward to see for himself why his tanks were disappearing into the sugarcane fields and were out of communication.

Sometime earlier, three Pakistani RCL Jeeps during a reconnaissance had mistakenly entered the battalion-defended area of 4 Grenadiers. The crews of two of these Jeeps were killed by the battalion's jawans but the third Jeep managed to get away. The jawans received a thorough dressing-down from their young company officer for allowing the third Jeep to get away and were told that in future, they were to hold their fire and not open fire without orders.

So, when the Pakistani GOC 1st Armoured Division along with his R Group drove into one of the company-defended localities of 4 Grenadiers, the soldiers did not fire. One of them stood up. The GOC, thinking he was still in his own area, asked the soldier to come up to him. On the soldier refusing to obey his orders, the GOC got down from his Jeep and started reaching for his pistol. This was too much for the Indian soldiers to accept and notwithstanding the orders not to fire, they opened fire on the Pakistani GOC and his group. The Commander Artillery Brigadier Shammi and all the occupants of the vehicles were killed but the GOC's R Group managed to drive away. After a few minutes, a message on the GOC's Rover (radio set) was intercepted. It said, *'Bara Imam mara gaya* (The Chief is no more).' The GOC's R Group had been escorted by armour. These tanks formed a protective shield around the body of the GOC, which was taken away by personnel of the R Group. The battalion, by this time, had run short of RCL ammunition and was subjected to heavy fire.

The body of Brigadier A.R. Shammi, Commander Pakistani Artillery of Pakistan's 1st Armoured Division and the others were recovered and buried according to the religious rites of the enemy. The Pakistani GOC's gorget patches (collar patches indicating a general's rank) were also found lying on the spot. The captured documents revealed the entire plan of Pakistan's Strike Corps which envisaged a quick advance and deep penetration into Indian territory up to Harike Bridge, Beas and Amritsar—an ambitious plan—which thus far had been thwarted by 4 Grenadiers and its stalwart CQMH Abdul Hamid. More action was to follow in one of the momentous tank battles fought between India and Pakistan at Asal Uttar.

While the astonishing drama in the location of 4 Grenadiers was drawing to a close, the curtain was lifting on an even more amazing battle between the armoured elements of the Indian and Pakistani armies in the area of Asal Uttar–Khem Karan and Patti.

Postscript

1. Abdul Hamid was recommended for and awarded the Param Vir Chakra, India's highest award for courage, when at risk to his life, he single-handedly destroyed three Pakistani Patton tanks. Subsequent to the announcement of the award, CQMH Abdul Hamid destroyed four more Patton tanks and died in the attempt. Perhaps it was a deserving case for the award of a bar to his PVC?
2. The Commanding Officer, Lt Col Farhat Bhatty, VSM, MiD, and his brave young officers deserve full credit for the outstanding performance of his battalion against overwhelming enemy forces, that too without his company commanders—his first tier of leadership.
3. The badges of rank of the Pakistani Commander Artillery Brigade and the gorget patches of the General Officer Commanding Pakistan's 1st Armoured Division can be seen in the War Museum of 4 Infantry Division.
4. The conduct of Abdul Hamid conveys emphatically how a single individual can contribute to victory in war.

4

Asal Uttar

Jai Jawan! Jai Kisan!

On 5 August 1965, Pakistan launched Operation Gibraltar, a guerrilla offensive to subvert the people of the state of Jammu and Kashmir. It followed up with Operation Grand Slam on 1 September, to sandwich Akhnur between a massive thrust of armour and infantry from the front and guerrillas from the rear.

Due to the overwhelming strength of the Pakistani offensive and the paucity of Indian troops in the area of Chhamb, Operation Grand Slam made substantial progress and Akhnur was under threat. It was at this stage that Raksha Mantri Shri Yashwantrao Chavan and Prime Minister Lal Bahadur Shastri came into the picture. The Indian Prime Minister had earlier on desired that the Indian armed forces should not extend the war, but faced with this impasse, he ordered the opening of the 'second front' in Punjab.

This decision by the Indian Prime Minister took the Pakistani military hierarchy by surprise. General Ayub Khan, President and Army Chief of Pakistan, mistakenly thought India would restrict the war to the boundaries of J & K as had earlier happened in the war of 1947–48. This, despite the Indian Prime Minister making it clear that if Pakistan attacked India in J & K, India would respond at a time and place of her own choosing.

The Indian operation in Punjab opened with India's XI Corps offensive to threaten Lahore from the south and the south-east. Unlike Pakistan's offensive forces, India's offensive force was infantry-heavy, which denied it the mobility that an armoured force could provide.

The crossing of the international border by the Indian Army early on the morning of 6 September caught the Pakistani defences off-guard and the Indian units and formations of XI Corps made rapid progress. However, the Pakistanis soon recovered from this setback and managed to stabilize their defences along the Ichhogil Canal. By the next day, it managed to blunt the Indian offensive using heavy artillery concentrations and the Pakistani Air Force.

Both armies, Indian and Pakistan, were adept at taking on unforeseen situations by 'contingency planning'. The Pakistan Army now put into practice their contingency plan to thwart the Indian offensive in the Kasur Sector, which was designed to threaten Lahore and outflank it from the south.

Having stalled the Indian offensive by the evening of 7 September, GOC 11 Pakistani Infantry Division, Major General Abdul Hamid, was directed to counter-attack, capture Khem Karan and establish a bridgehead in that area, to allow Pakistan's 1 Armoured Division to break out and advance towards Amritsar and the Beas River. General Musa, the Pakistani Army Chief, and the Pakistan high command were, at that stage, uncertain of the location of India's 1 Armoured Division, which was part of India's Strike Force, and they had no option but to go on the offensive themselves.[1]

The Indian planners were aware that Pakistan would react violently to its offensive in Punjab. They too, had their own contingency plans and decided to switch from the offensive to 'offensive defence', so as to destroy the Pakistani Strike Force, particularly, its armour complement. It was decided that Asal Uttar would be a more suitable place to destroy the enemy offensive, rather than Khem Karan, which could be bypassed. Asal Uttar covered both the Khem Karan–Amritsar axis as well as the Khem Karan–Patti axis.

The Pakistani 1st Armoured Division attacked on 10 September, exactly as anticipated by the Indians and attempted to break out, but they first had to destroy the defences of the 4th Grenadiers. The battalion held on with great determination and upset the Pakistani time plan. The issue now for the Indians was to get the Indian armoured and infantry units and formations into their defended locations in the area of Asal Uttar–Khem Karan–Patti in time, to meet and destroy the Pakistani threat.

Meanwhile, between 6 and 8 September, India's 4 Infantry Division held on to their defended area despite the repeated armour-backed assaults that attempted to dislodge them so that the Pakistani armoured division could break out from the area of Khem Karan towards Amritsar and the Beas River.

Quantitatively and qualitatively the armour component of the Pakistani offensive was of a higher calibre.[2] They had six armoured regiments as part of 3, 4 and 5 Armoured Brigades. In addition, 10 and 11 Pakistani Infantry divisions had armoured regiments integral to their divisions. This made the tank-to-tank ratio between Pakistan and India 4:1. Also Pakistani tanks were mostly M-47 and M-48 Pattons which were far superior to the antiquated Shermans and Centurions of the Indian armoured regiments. The Centurions, however, were able to take on the Pattons, but the Shermans were totally outclassed.

By this time, Pakistan's top secret master plan for its 'Thrust to the Beas' fell into Indian hands through marked maps and orders left behind in an abandoned tank, which gave the Indians not only the full Pakistani ORBAT (Order of Battle)[3] but also the detailed plan of the offensive that included aims, objectives, phases, groupings, tasks, timings, bounds, administration and logistics of the Pakistani armoured and infantry formations.

M-48 Patton, Pakistan's main battle tank

Pakistan's 5 Armoured Brigade under Brigadier Bashir planned a two-pronged drive by both his armoured regiments 24 Cavalry and 6 Lancers as under:

a. 24 Cavalry with one company of 1 Frontier Force, code-named 'Group Ali' to outflank Khem Karan from the west with the aim of cutting the Khem Karan–Bhikhiwind axis at Chima.
b. 6 Lancer's Alpha Squadron with another company of 1 Frontier Force code-named 'Group Gul' to move on the Khem Karan–Patti axis with the aim of capturing Valtoha.
c. Squadrons from 6 and 15 Lancers with the remaining companies of 1 Frontier Force code-named 'Group Shabbir' to be the Brigade Reserve with the task of capturing HQ 4 Infantry Division and the GOC.

The Pakistani plan could only be countered if Brigadier Theogaraj, Commander 2 (I) Armoured Brigade could get his armoured regiments and infantry components to the defensive layout that he and his armoured regimental commanders had earlier planned. Unfortunately for him, GOC XI Corps had detached 3 Cavalry from his command and placed it as a reserve of XI Corps for the defensive battle at Dera Baba Nanak. His brigade was left only with Deccan Horse.

Brigadier Theogaraj, Salim Caleb and Arun Vaidya, commandants of 3 Cavalry and Deccan Horse respectively, had war-gamed various scenarios based on the terrain and the possible strength of enemy armour, and had come to the conclusion that the enemy thrust line would develop on the Bhikhiwind axis through Khem Karan. This was in keeping with the grain of the country, i.e., the pattern and texture of the ground. The Rohi Nullah to the west and the Sutlej River to the east would protect the flanks of the Pakistani offensive. They believed, however, that the enemy offensive could be contained and destroyed where room for manoeuvre was limited, and that happened to be in the area of Asal Uttar–Chima.

Time was running out. Salim Caleb, Commandant 3 Cavalry, was aware that he was in the wrong place and that there was a critical need for his regiment to be in the defensive layout to stem the Pakistani offensive heading for Amritsar and the Beas. At that juncture, Deccan Horse was alone and heavily outnumbered. He knew that this was the moment of destiny for his regiment and for India. Caleb therefore decided to move his regiment to Khem Karan without orders, in order to reach the place where he knew he was most needed, to be part of a tank battle—which eventually would turn out to be one of the greatest tank battles since World War II.

He ordered 'B' Squadron commanded by Major 'Belu' Belvalkar to dash at full speed towards Asal Uttar and 'A' Squadron commanded by Major Suresh Chander Vadera to move post-haste on the Valtoha–Patti axis. His regimental headquarters and 'C' Squadron followed hard on the heels of Belvalkar's squadron. The regiment covered the distance from Bhikhiwind in under two hours and both squadrons deployed in their battle formations just in time, prior to the Pakistani offensive. The arrival of the Centurions of 3 Cavalry was a big morale booster to the beleaguered 4 Mountain Division. Caleb met Vaidya who brought him up to date on the tactical situation. Both commanding officers coordinated all details for the upcoming battle.[4]

In the meantime, Alpha and Bravo squadrons of India's Deccan Horse along with the infantry elements of 7 and 62 Mountain Brigade deployed to halt the Pakistani armoured thrust. Alpha squadron was tasked to stay in contact with the Pakistanis and halt the advance of its armour. Keeping in the middle of the Bhikhiwind–Khem Karan axis, Major Jimmy Vohra got his tanks into position using the trees and sugarcane plantations as cover. Bravo squadron took position to the south of Asal Uttar on the Patti–Valtoha axis. These two squadrons formed the tip of the southern arm of the Indian 'horseshoe defences' planned to take on the Pakistani advancing armour.

As the Pakistani Pattons advanced, the tanks of Deccan Horse knocked out eleven Pattons. The Pattons broke contact and made a hurried withdrawal after suffering these heavy losses. Alpha squadron Deccan Horse lost four tanks: three destroyed and one bogged down. Deccan Horse had won the first round, but the battle was just beginning.[5]

Meanwhile, the IAF, on 6 September itself, was carrying out its tasks of interdiction to assist the ground forces by destroying the threat at Dera Baba Nanak (DBN), thus freeing 3 Cavalry to take on its rightful role in the area of Asal Uttar. In this operation, the IAF destroyed ten or twelve Pattons that were heading for the DBN bridge. On 8 September, air strikes by the IAF Hunters destroyed an ammunition-laden train and a large number of vehicles in the Raiwind marshalling yard and some tanks in the Kasur Sector that were moving to reinforce the Pakistani armoured brigades. Again, on 9 September, Mysteres of the IAF launched crippling strikes on a tank-transporting train, destroying and damaging more than twenty tanks. Faced with these losses of tanks and ammunition, Pakistan's 1 Armoured Division moved back to await further orders.

Meanwhile Brigadier Theogaraj, his armoured regimental commanders and the infantry elements of 4 Indian Infantry Division reorganized their defences and worked on a plan to destroy the armoured brigades of Pakistan's 1 Armoured Division. The brigade occupied a horseshoe formation of defence. Tanks and tank-hunting teams were well concealed and were supported by artillery in coordination with infantry anti-tank recoilless guns. The defenders waited in anticipation for the inevitable Pakistani assault that was to follow.

Brigadier Theogaraj, Commander 2 Independent Armoured Brigade, was given the following tasks:

- In general, prevent enemy armour from bypassing the division-defended sector, 4 Infantry Division
- In particular, prevent enemy armour ingress north or south of the division sector; deploy armour to prevent Pakistani armour thrusts through gaps in the Valtoha–Bahadur Nagar area and the area of Asal Uttar–Mastgarh; and inflict maximum attrition on enemy armour.[6]
- 'Pakistani plans from the highest to the lowest in the Khem Karan sector had been made on maps.

> They obviously did not have information of local factors of the terrain nor had the seasons been taken into account.'[7]

The water table in the Khem Karan Sector was particularly high in September after the monsoon, with water seeping off slowly into drains and the Sutlej River at its south-east extremity. This was not the season to launch a major armoured force into this region. December to January or April to May was the perfect time.[8]

To plan an armoured advance in the Khem Karan Sector as well as the direction the forces were to follow along major canals and drains was professional ignorance.[9]

In the meanwhile, the Punjabi farmers were persuaded to leave their fields before the impending battle. Unsure of what would happen, the farmers broke the irrigation bunds so that their fields would get the required water during their absence. This helped the defenders, as the Pakistani Pattons got bogged down in the soggy soil, enabling Indian tank-hunting teams, anti-tank guns, artillery and armour to pick out the stranded Pattons and destroy them as they converged into the killing ground prepared for them. At this time, the Indian Army had no clue that Pakistan had another armoured division (6 Armoured Division) waiting in the wings to be used at the right moment. This division was held back and not used because the Pakistanis did not know the whereabouts of India's 1 Armoured Division and whether it would be used in the Sialkot Sector or in Punjab. Not using this army reserve proved to be a strategic failure of the Pakistani high command.

Abdul Hamid's RCL gun versus Pakistani Pattons

The holding back of the Indian 2 (I) Armoured Brigade also puzzled the Pakistanis who did not know why it was not being used in an offensive role. It was not known to them that this brigade was, in fact, waiting for them in the Asal Uttar–Khem Karan–Patti area.

The history of 4 Mountain Division states:

> The Deccan Horse and heavy concentration by our artillery helped in keeping the enemy at bay for some

time, but the weight of the enemy attack was such that its very momentum pushed a large number of his tanks within the killing range of the battalions. At this juncture the RCL gunners of the Rajputana Rifles helped by those of the J and K Rifles excelled each other in their marksmanship. At least ten tanks were destroyed or disabled.

The war diary of 9 Horse (Deccan Horse) for 9 September says:

The enemy having probed and found out the extent of our defences started its offensive towards Beas and Harike by advancing in three columns along Asal Uttar-Valtoha track (opposite B Squadron) in the centre, and along road Khem Karan towards Cheema (A Squadron's positions). A fierce tank versus tank battle ensued in which 9 enemy tanks were knocked out – 5 by A Squadron and 4 by B Squadron. The advance of the enemy was effectively stemmed. Two troops of C Squadron under 2/Lt TS Shergill and RHQ were employed to protect the gun area. Some enemy infantry which had managed to infiltrate was shot up by RHQ under Lt GS Randhawa.

It would be recalled that Brigadier A.R. Shammi, the Commander Artillery of Pakistan's 1 Armoured Division, was killed within the battalion-defended area of 4 Grenadiers, the details of which have been narrated in the story of CQMH Abdul Hamid. From the maps and documents recovered from the brigadier's jeep, it was seen that the enemy had drawn up grandiose plans to advance up to the Amritsar–Jalandhar portion of the GT Road via Harike in three columns, cutting the road south of Amritsar at Jandiala and at Beas.

The plans of the three groups—Group Ali, Group Gul and Group Shabbir of 5 Armoured Brigade—came to naught. Brigadier Bashir was later removed from command because of the poor performance of his brigade where morale was obviously low, as tank after tank were abandoned by their crew.

4 Cavalry of 4 Armoured Brigade surrendered en masse led by their commanding officer Lt Col Nazir on the pretext that his tanks had run out of fuel. This was proved false as the tanks were driven off by drivers of Deccan Horse and 3 Cavalry. Some still had their engines running while the others started up without difficulty and were driven off. Some more, which had got bogged down, were later recovered. This marked the end of 4 Cavalry. It proved beyond doubt that 4 Cavalry had lost the will to fight. 4 Cavalry had disintegrated and ceased to exist as a unit. The commander of 4 Armoured Brigade, Brigadier Lumb, was also removed from command. GOC 1st Armoured Division, Maj. Gen. Nasir Ahmed, was sacked on 18 September. The reason for the sackings was the breakdown of command and control resulting in the collapse of morale of the division and the brigades. The only commander to survive was Brigadier Moin-ud-Din of 3 Armoured Brigade that had moved out to the Sialkot Sector on 10/11 September.

Having lost the ability to continue the offensive any further, Pakistan's high command called off the offensive and pulled out the remnants of Pakistan's 1 Armoured Division to meet the threat of India's I Corps offensive in the Sialkot Sector.

The ability of the Indian Army to quickly change from an offensive to a defensive role helped in the destruction of the Pakistani armoured division at Asal Uttar. After the ceasefire, Asal Uttar became known as 'Patton Nagar' due to the large number of destroyed Patton tanks that lay strewn all over the area.

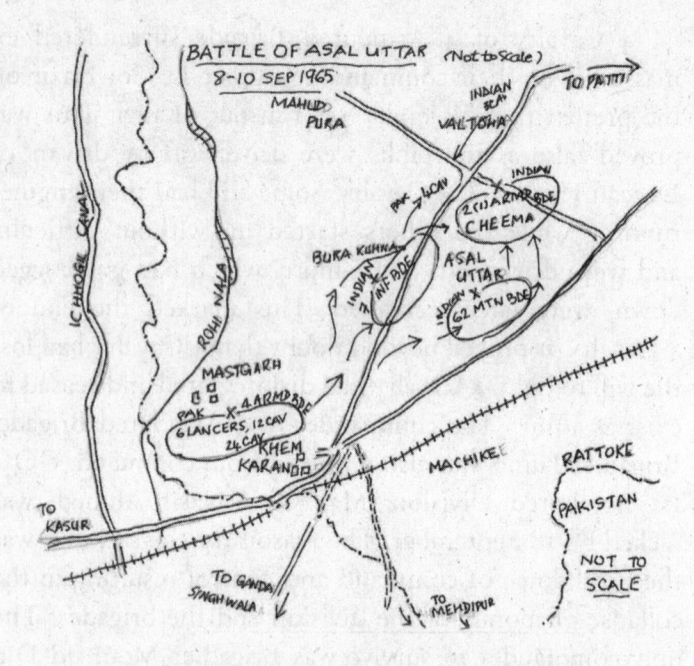

The Battle of Asal Uttar, Indo–Pakistan War of 1965, Ministry of Defence, Govt of India, between pages 160 and 161, New Delhi, 2011

Postscript

1. The battle of Asal Uttar proved to be one of the greatest tank battles after World War II where an offensive by a Pakistani armoured division was held and destroyed by an Indian armoured brigade. A total of ninety-seven Patton tanks were lost by Pakistan, of which thirty-two were in good running condition and captured by Indian troops.

2. Brigadier A.R. Shammi, Commander Artillery of Pakistan's 1st Armoured Division, was killed in the battalion-defended area of 4 Grenadiers and the GOC of the division was wounded but escaped capture.
3. Sixty-four more Pattons were destroyed in the battles of Phillaura and Chawinda in the Sialkot Sector, making a total of 131 Pattons destroyed in this war out of the 400 Pattons gifted to the Pakistanis by the Americans.
4. Napoleon's offensive towards Stalingrad was destroyed by snow and frost. Similarly, it was slush and mud that ground the Pakistani offensive to a dismal defeat.
5. The Indian Army could have done much better in this war, but the troops were raw. I Corps and 6 Mountain Division had been raised just four months before the war. Most units had not had the time to do collective training after being raised before the war. Their training, therefore, was incomplete. Notwithstanding this, the units and formations fought and delivered despite some hiccups. The experience of this war emphatically emphasizes the importance of training—a crucial lesson for the future! Although the manner in which the Pakistani offensive rolled out was anticipated, the benefit of those war games appeared to have been lost during the prelude to the war.
6. In addition to the failure of the grandiose Pakistani plans to reach the Beas River, it became clear that

the armoured division and brigade commanders of the Pakistan Army had lost the will to fight—the armoured division commander and two of the armoured brigade commanders were sacked and an armoured regiment disintegrated and ceased to exist.

7. 4 Grenadiers had destroyed fifteen Pattons with their recoilless anti-tank guns and handheld anti-tank weapons. It had held its ground despite being under constant armoured threat and without the leadership of its company commanders who had taken over command responsibility of an operational sector elsewhere. The battalion was awarded the battle honour of 'Asal Uttar' and the Theatre Honour of 'Punjab 1965', in addition to the Param Vir Chakra awarded to CQMH Abdul Hamid.

8. 2 (I) Armoured Brigade, Deccan Horse and 3 Cavalry fought with distinction in the battle of Asal Uttar. All three commanders were awarded the MVC—India's second-highest award for courage in battle.

9. The dreams of the Pakistani high command to encircle the holy city of Amritsar came to naught. The Pakistani offensive had been launched for the wrong strategic reasons, in the wrong region and the wrong season.

10. There were major differences between India's Western Army Commander Lt Gen. Harbakhsh Singh and the Army Chief Gen. Chaudhry on how the war was to be fought in the XI Corps Zone. Fortunately, better sense prevailed and differences were resolved, resulting in an unprecedented victory.
11. Many historians seem to think that the Indo–Pak war was a stalemate. This is not true. It is generally accepted that victory goes to the side that destroys the enemy war machine and its will to continue the fight. By this parameter, it can be safely said that India won the Indo–Pak war of 1965.

Graveyard of Pakistani Pattons

Asal Uttar

5

Chhamb Battleground[1]

'Good decisions come from experience. But experience also comes from bad decisions. This is life. So, never regret but learn from mistakes and go ahead.'

—Anonymous

Brigadier Behram Master, Commander 191 Indian Infantry Brigade, was in the hill sector at Dewa, giving orders to his 'O' Group[2] when a Pakistani helicopter spotted them and asked for artillery fire on the Indians. An artillery round landed on an ammunition dump located within the post and the resultant explosion killed the brigadier and several of his officers. Dewa was a post that overlooked the Chhamb plains. This occurred on 15 August 1965 at 1000 hours. War had not been declared, but such issues did not matter to the Pakistan Army. The Indians were not aware that the artillery shelling on that day was but a prelude for something much bigger.

Chhamb had been a battleground between India and Pakistan in the Indo–Pak war of 1947–48 and would figure in most of the wars fought between the two countries thereafter. Chhamb is strategically important to both India and Pakistan and that is why it has been a common denominator of all the wars we have fought with Pakistan—except Kargil.

Chhamb can be used as a launch pad by India to access important strategic objectives in Pakistan. The Marala Headworks lie within striking distance from the international border (IB) as well as from the Cease-Fire Line, both of which lie ahead of Chhamb. There is also Hardinge Bridge, over the Chenab River, which if destroyed or even damaged, can choke the Strike Forces of the Pakistan Army and prevent them from carrying out their assigned roles in areas of vital importance to their security. The area west of Chhamb is ideal tank country, with plenty of scope for manoeuvre for mobile forces.

For Pakistan, Chhamb is important because it provides a base for an approach to Akhnur, the capture of which could threaten the lifeline to Rajouri, Naushera and Poonch and thereafter the alternate route to the Srinagar Valley via the Pir Panjal. The capture of Akhnur would also threaten Jammu, a town of strategic and political importance to India.

The ground on our side of the border in Chhamb is in the shape of an inverted triangle with the base of the triangle on the Munawar Tawi River with the area narrowing down to its apex resting on the Akhnur Bridge. The two sides of this isosceles triangle are the Chenab River on one side and the Kalidhar hills on the other, which give protection to the flanks of any attacking force. Whereas the ground configuration is good for an offensive, the defence, if properly planned, is equally good for a strong defensive battle.

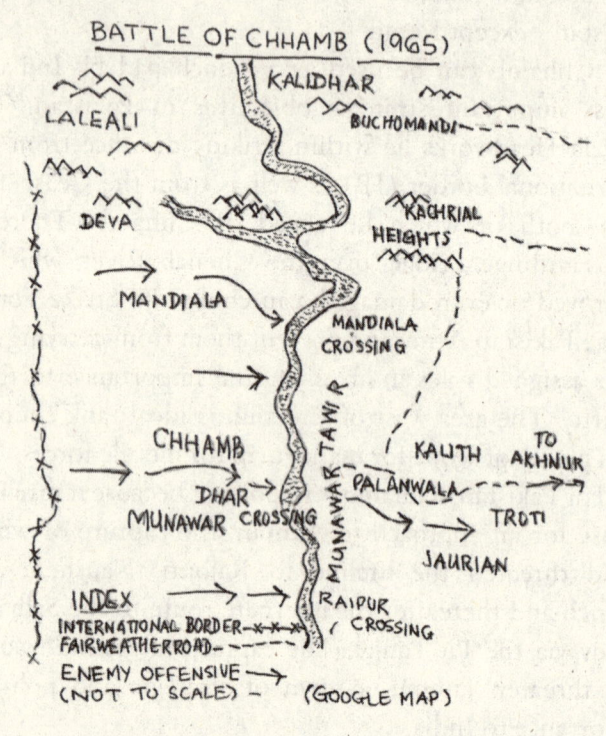

Battle of Chhamb: Area of operations

Our forces holding Chhamb consisted of just one infantry brigade with one of its battalions in the hill sector on the Kalidhar Ridge and three battalions in the plains. For armour, it had just one squadron of light AMX tanks from

20 Lancers, and a field regiment and a medium battery for artillery support.

It is strange that notwithstanding the strategic importance of the Chhamb Sector, not enough significance was given to the planning of its defence in the Indian Army's overall strategic plan in 1965. This, despite the war games held in 1956–57 and 1958–59 and in subsequent discussions held at Headquarters Western Command Shimla, which highlighted the vulnerability of Chhamb and its strategic importance. Although the Army Commander, Lt Gen. Harbakhsh Singh, subsequently accepted that the capture of Chhamb could be an objective, the Corps Commander Lt Gen. K.C. Katoch obdurately felt otherwise. Pakistan, on the other hand, appreciated the vital and strategic importance of Akhnur and allocated a formidable offensive force of an infantry division that included two infantry brigades in the assault role and one in the holding role, with another infantry division in reserve, two armoured regiments, two medium artillery regiments, three field regiments, two batteries of heavy artillery, one locating regiment, one locating battery and one light anti-aircraft battery.

Pakistan's offensive plan for the capture of Akhnur was code-named Operation Grand Slam.

Our intelligence agencies finally began to wake up to the enemy force build-up opposite Chhamb. All earlier information received from them focused on Operation Gibraltar. The first intelligence report relating to Chhamb was received on 14 August. It reported, for the first time, that enemy forces had concentrated at Moel. This was immediately followed up with a report indicating the move of a squadron of tanks to Mattewala opposite Chhamb. During this time, the infiltrators had attacked the police station at Palanwala. 3 Mahar chased and captured fourteen of them and killed four.

191 Infantry Brigade was at this time without a Brigade Commander. Finally, Brig. Manmohan Singh, who was commanding a brigade in 26 Infantry Division, was moved to take over 191 Infantry. Being new to his task, he had little or no knowledge of the brigade. HQ 10 Infantry Division was, at this time, under raising in Bangalore and Belgaum. It was now tasked to move to J & K to take over 191 and 80 Infantry Brigades in the Chhamb and Jhangar Sectors. When Pakistan launched Operation Grand Slam on 1 September 1965, Maj. Gen. D.B. Chopra, GOC 10 Infantry Division was on his first visit to 80 Infantry Brigade at Jhangar to begin to learn the contours of his command. He was immediately ordered to assume command of the Chhamb–Jaurian Sector, although according to previous orders, 191 Infantry Brigade was to come under the command of 10 Infantry Division only by 15 September 1965. The Pakistan Army, however, was many steps ahead of the Indian Army and launched its offensive on 1 September, giving no time for 10 Infantry Division to get its act together.

This was the shabby manner in which the defence of the Chhamb battle of 1965 was planned and organized. Worse still, units of medium artillery allotted to 191 Infantry Brigade were taken away by XV Corps and allotted to the Poonch Sector.[3]

It appears that very little attention had been paid to the deliberations of the earlier war games that had highlighted the threat to Chhamb and HQ XV Corps failed to make contingency plans to anticipate that threat. The command and control of 10 Infantry Division was in poor shape to take on an offensive as big as Operation Grand Slam. GOC XV Corps, Lt Gen. K.S. Katoch, continued to insist that Chhamb was less likely to be attacked by Pakistan and that it was the Jhangar Sector that was more likely to be under threat.[4] The attack on Chhamb proved how wrong he was.

On 25 August, the Army Commander, Lt Gen. Harbakhsh Singh gave out his appreciation of the situation.[5] He believed that Pakistan would launch her main offensive across the CFL with large-scale infiltration using irregular forces. This would be followed up with a full-scale attack in the Chhamb Sector but he did not believe that Akhnur would be Pakistan's main objective. This, despite authentic information from Maj. Gen. Thapan, GOC 26 Infantry Division, and United Nations observers that there was a heavy concentration of troops, including armour in the vicinity of Chhamb. This could only mean that Chhamb was under threat and that Akhnur could be a likely Pakistani objective.

Brig. Manmohan Singh took command of 191 Infantry Brigade on 16 August, about a fortnight after Brig. Behram Master had been killed. On taking over, he learnt that the brigade held a huge frontage that included both the international border (IB) and the CFL, and it was held by four infantry battalions.

When he took command, ten posts had been vacated due to heavy Pakistani artillery fire. By 24 August, the new Brigade Commander had recovered all the posts.

Despite all information to the contrary, Gen. Katoch had, with regard to the 10 Division Sector, given his appreciation that 'It is not considered that Pakistani build-up is significant to launch any major offensive against this sector. The main threat in the future is likely to consist of:

1. Continued attempts by irregulars to infiltrate into the interior and raid headquarters, maintenance routes and administrative areas, and
2. Shelling of forward posts, troop and vehicle concentrations and own gun areas within their artillery range.'[6]

Brigadier Manmohan Singh

Brig. Manmohan Singh was weary of the stubborn insistence by XV Corps Headquarters that there was no significant threat to the Chhamb Sector despite feedback from various sources that a large contingent of Patton tanks had congregated opposite Chhamb. Even at this point, Gen. Katoch continued to be in denial. 'It gives a fair idea of how things were at the higher headquarters. Nobody wanted to even listen, leave alone give credibility to anything, no matter how consequential or important it might be, if it did not fit in with their way of thinking.'[7]

Gen. Katoch, instead of listening to Brig. Manmohan Singh, a forward field commander, told Gen. Chopra, GOC 10 Infantry Division, 'Brigadier Manmohan Singh,

Commander 191 Infantry Brigade Group, is totally new to the sector and operational developments, having assumed command on 16 August. He is inclined to be "jittery" and tends to "cry wolf". On the basis of a few reports rendered by forward troops of heavy infantry and artillery concentration opposite his sector, the Brigade Commander has been voicing his apprehension of an imminent Pakistani attack in strength in his sector.'

Chopra was cautioned to ignore this tendency as there was no threat to this sector and infiltration had already been contained. The corps had no plans to prepare defensive positions east of the Munawar Tawi. Based on this assessment, even anti-tank mines were denied to 191 Infantry Brigade.[8]

Gen. Dharam Bir Chopra and his GSO 1 were told to report to HQ Western Command on 25 August 1965. Generals Harbakhsh Singh and Kashmir Katoch were both present and the army commander gave out his appreciation of the situation.

On 26 August, HQ XV Corps ordered GOC 10 Infantry Division to set up his HQ at Akhnur by 29 August along with a skeletal staff.

Sometime near the end of August, Gen. Harbakhsh conceded that he may have been mistaken in his earlier appreciation and that there could be some armour in the vicinity of Chhamb. He sent a specific signal to Lt Gen. Katoch to take adequate measures to defend Chhamb as follows:

From GOC-in-C for GOC (.) recommend for your consideration holding of bridgehead covering Chhamb and Mandiala crossing with minimum two battalions against any thrust by Pak regular troops supported by armour from direction southwest even if it means thinning out border posts.[9]

It, however, transpires that no action was taken on this signal.

Maj. Rusty Dey of 2 Lancers, the Brigade Major of HQ 191 Infantry Brigade, informed HQ XV Corps of the fact that he had gone across the border and seen for himself evidence of Pakistani armour opposite Chhamb. The staff officer of XV Corps refused to believe him, till Maj. Dey in exasperation said, 'Damn it, don't tell me, an armoured corps officer, that I don't recognize tank tracks.'[10]

Brig. Jogindar Singh, in his book *Behind the Scene*, gives out his reasons why he felt that Pakistan would launch an offensive in this sector:

a. The approach provided direct access to the Akhnur Bridge, the capture of which would strangle the lifeline of 25 Infantry Division to Naushera–Rajouri–Poonch.
b. It was the only area where Pakistan could use its armour and heavy artillery. Flanks of the offensive would be protected by the Chenab River on the right side and the low hills and broken ground on the left.
c. Pakistan's approach into this area provided easy logistic support. Reinforcements to feed the offensive from its established administrative bases would be quicker, safer and easier to maintain the momentum of the thrust once the battle was joined.

According to UN restrictions, India could only reinforce the Chhamb Sector from within the quantum of troops permitted in J & K. Diversion of any force into the Chhamb Sector would automatically weaken other areas in J & K. Pakistan suffered from no such handicap. In addition, the Chenab River was a big obstacle against quick reinforcement by India, particularly in bringing up armour and medium artillery.[11]

The defensive layout of 191 Infantry Brigade had 15 Kumaon along with the Brigade HQ at Mandiala, 6 Sikh LI deployed along the CFL from Bure Jal to Pir Jamal, 3 Mahar with elements of 3 J & K Militia north of Pir Jamal and 6/5 GR (FF) holding the hill sector at Kalidhar.

Although 191 Infantry Brigade would come under the command of 10 Infantry Division only by 15 September, Gen. Chopra advised Commander 191 Infantry Brigade to have properly prepared defences east of the Munawar Tawi along the line Kalit–Troti–Jaurian. This made sense, but the Pakistani attack on 1 September had jumped the gun and did not give the brigade any time to carry out this sound suggestion.

Major Bhaskar Roy, Squadron Commander 20 Lancers

Maj. Bhaskar Roy, Commander 'C' Squadron 20 Lancers, had 14 AMX-13 tanks under his command. These were light tanks with armour that was 40 mm thick and a 75 mm gun that had an effective range of just 500 yards. These were no match for the Pakistani M-48 Pattons that had a 90 mm gun with a range of 1500 yards and armour protection that was 120 mm thick. Bhaskar Roy's tanks were outclassed even before the war had begun but Bhaskar resolved to battle it out as best as he could. He moved his tanks forward to take on the Pattons at close range. Earlier to the Pakistani offensive, in his appreciation of how the enemy armour would advance, Maj. Roy had shared with Brig. Manmohan Singh and Maj. Rusty Dey that he expected the Pakistani armour to cross the border from the IB side rather than the CFL side because the ground was more conducive to movement by armour.[12] In anticipation of the offensive, Bhaskar Roy made his plans, identifying areas from where his AMX tanks could take on the Pattons from well-camouflaged locations.

1 September 1965, 0330 hours

In the early hours of the morning of 1 September, Pakistan launched Operation Grand Slam with a concentrated onslaught of artillery fire, the weight of which had never before been witnessed by Indian troops. The ground literally shook and reverberated with the weight of artillery fire, which tore apart the bunkers and decimated the defenders. The bombardment aimed at destroying the defenders continued for two and a half hours and the tremors could be felt in faraway Jammu, so heavy was the fall of artillery fire. The fire support that was made available to Operation Grand Slam was unprecedented in subcontinental history. A total of nine field batteries, seven medium batteries and two heavy batteries added up to 110 guns firing in unison to support the Pakistani assaulting infantry brigades.

The barrage was followed by two regiments of Pattons and Shermans that overran the trenches of the defenders. Those survivors who were not blown apart by the artillery or overrun by Pakistani armour confronted the advancing infantry and took them on with their small arms.

The tank-to-tank battle

Maj. Bhaskar Roy, standing on his seat of his tank, had half of his body outside of the cupola of his tank. He looked at the advancing mass of Pattons and Shermans and realized what he was up against. He could have withdrawn against such overwhelming odds, but that was not an option for him. Indian counter bombardment was non-existent, the Indian gun positions having taken their own share of the pounding, and there were no anti-tank mines, because HQ XV Corps had refused to accept that Pakistan armour would be committed to this sector. Outgunned almost 6 to 1, Roy prepared as best as he could, by splitting the squadron into troops of three tanks and spacing them over a considerable distance to counter the massive spread of the advancing Pattons. His plan was to use the better manoeuvrability of his light AMX tanks and to wait for the advancing Pattons to come within firing range, then fire and move to another position to fire again to make the effort appear bigger than it was. Roy's tactics were highly successful and by late afternoon, 'C' Squadron had disabled more than 15 Pakistani Pattons.[13]

It was seen that Pakistani armour suffered heavy casualties at the hands of Roy's squadron and the recoilless rifles of the Indian infantry. Shaukat Riza, a Pakistan historian confirms this. He says:

Alpha squadron with 9 Punjab reached south of Chhamb at about 0900 hours. Five of our tanks were hit by enemy recoilless rifles. They had been very well-sited to cover tank runs. Charlie squadron made contact with Dalla post at about 0700 hours. In a sharp engagement, the squadron lost three tanks . . . the squadron lost most of its tanks in engaging Chak Pandit. Raza Shah did not look back . . . a few hundred yards short of Chak Pandit, his was the only running tank on the scene . . . at about 0900 hours an enemy recoilless rifle hit it on the side . . . the tank exploded.[14]

Bhaskar Roy lost his first troop leader, the fearless twenty-one-year-old Second Lieutenant Ravi Laroia, very early in the battle. It was well known that the Mandiala Heights across the Munawar Tawi would be an important objective both for the attacker and the defender. Realizing this, Laroia volunteered to hold this important feature against the assaulting enemy, fully aware that this would be a perilous mission. Bhaskar watched him racing with his troop to get to this ridge before the Pattons could get there. He watched him reach the ridge successfully only to see him blown up by murderous fire from the Pattons.

Bhaskar Roy now moved his tank to a more commanding position to direct the tank battle. He did so standing out of his tank's turret, in full view of the enemy, his tank's pennants indicating that he was the commander, fearlessly directing the battle visually, rather than from the safety of the inside of the tank's turret. By late evening, four more of his tanks were destroyed and his own tank was hit, decapitating the gunner and killing his driver. He continued to direct the battle from another tank.

Pakistani Pattons attacking Indian infantry at Chhamb

The Pakistani grand plan

Aware of the devastation caused by the preponderance of artillery fire from his guns, Maj. Gen. Akhtar Hussain Malik, GOC 12 Pakistani Infantry Division, moved his Tactical HQ to Kharian. He had planned to carry out his offensive in three phases. In phase 1, he planned to destroy all infantry opposition on the western side of the Munawar Tawi. This included the capture of Dewa, Laleali, Sakrana and Chhamb by 1000 hours of Day 1. In phase 2, he planned to race towards Akhnur and capture the bridge over the Chenab by 1200 hours on the same day. Then he would use 7 Pakistani Infantry Division, commanded by Maj. Gen. Yahya Khan, to sweep northwards to capture Rajouri by 2 September as part of Phase 3. Nusrat Force of Operation Gibraltar was to continue its subversive activities in the areas of Rajouri, Naushera and Jhangar. The concept was to sandwich the Indian defenders between the assaulting Pakistani formations of Operation Grand Slam from the front and the guerrillas of Operation Gibraltar from the rear. As a concept, it was an ambitious plan, which did not reckon with other factors that would come in the way of his aim and objectives.

The employment of Pakistani artillery

Shaukat Riza, a Pakistani General and military historian, commented on the deployment and employment of Pakistani artillery. He wrote:

> The artillery plan for support of the battle was both bold and meticulous. Medium guns and 8-inch Howitzers (Heavy artillery) were deployed ahead of the field guns. This bold measure enabled our artillery to dominate the battlefield. Survey of guns, observation posts and targets were carried out in the preceding weeks without alerting the enemy. Gun positions were occupied during the night of 30/31 August. 4 Corps Artillery Brigade command post was established at Padhar. H hour was fixed at 0500 hours 1 September. At 0330 hours, on 1 September, 4 Corps and artillery 7 Division started preparatory bombardment. Targets at Deva, Barsala, Chhamb and across Tawi were hit with nine field, seven medium and two heavy batteries.[15]

The infantry battle

The ground offensive by Pakistan was launched at 0500 hours on 1 September. Phase 1 was launched with two infantry brigades attacking and one holding ground. The attacking brigades had two armoured regiments in support, along twin axes with 4 AK Brigade supported by 13 Lancers in the north and 102 Infantry Brigade with 11 Cavalry in the south. Troops from the holding brigade simultaneously attacked objectives in the Hill Sector, capturing some posts.

The devastating and concentrated Pakistani artillery fire that continued for two and a half hours, obliterated the Indian defences and by the end of the bombardment, the infantry positions were in a precarious state. As the artillery barrage lifted, the two Pakistani armoured regiments—13 Lancers and 11 Cavalry—advanced in support of the assaulting brigades. The surviving infantry soldiers of 6 Sikh LI and 3 Mahar continued to hold fast to their defences. As soon as the shelling stopped, these brave battalions took on the advancing Pakistani infantry and armour with their machine guns and RCL guns, causing heavy casualties to Pakistani armour and infantry.

Under the circumstances, the troops of 191 Infantry Brigade had displayed great grit and determination. However, faced with this overwhelming fire, half of 6 Sikh LI was wiped out. Brig. Manmohan Singh ordered Col. Nandagopal of 6 Sikh LI to fall back for the defence of Akhnur. In the meanwhile, 3 Mahar, commanded by Lt Col Gurbans Singh Sangha, continued to hold on to its beleaguered defences. Although the battalion had been reinforced by a company from 3 JAK Militia, it had no anti-tank mines. The CO sited his companies on high ground to prevent enemy armour from overrunning them. Brig. Manmohan Singh told Sangha to hang on and that artillery, armour and air support would soon come to their aid.[16] Colonel Sangha was subsequently awarded a Maha Vir Chakra for his bold and courageous leadership.

The air battle over Chhamb

Despite fierce resistance by the defenders, the infantry positions were falling one after another under the relentless pressure by the Pakistani juggernaut. 191 Indian Infantry Brigade now asked for air support at 1100 hours. Air support, however, required the sanction of the Government of India as it would mean escalation into an all-out war. The Army Chief, General Chaudhuri, however, was away from Army Headquarters and was able to reach Delhi only in the evening. He straightaway met Air Chief Marshal Arjan Singh and discussed the situation in Chhamb, and together they entered the office of Minister of Defence Shri Yashwantrao Chavan at 1630 hours, which was nearly five hours after Brig. Manmohan Singh had asked for air support.

In accordance with the rules of conduct, at that point of time, the Emergency Coordination Committee (ECC) was required to give the go-ahead for the use of air power, after the Prime Minister had given his assent. However, time was at a premium and the battle had reached a critical stage. There was no time to go to the ECC or to even make a call to the Prime Minister. The Raksha Mantri just said, 'Go ahead.' The time was 1650 hours![17]

Chhamb Battleground

Soon after the Raksha Mantri had sanctioned the use of air power, four Vampires were airborne and vectored on to Chhamb. At this time, the infantry of 191 Indian Infantry Brigade and a few AMX tanks of 20 Lancers were still holding the Pakistanis at bay. Brig. Manmohan Singh and the troops of 191 Indian Infantry Brigade were relieved to see the IAF over Chhamb. Unfortunately, the IAF aircraft, instead of attacking the Pakistani tanks and infantry, repeatedly attacked our own positions. When they did go for the Pakistani Pattons, they were met with a hail of anti-aircraft fire that hit one Vampire, which crashed to the ground.

The second wave of Vampires was over Chhamb after the first wave returned, but by now, the PAF were into the air battle. This wave was led by Squadron Leader (Sqn Ldr) Aspi Bhagwagar and comprised Flight Lieutenants (Flt Lts) Satish Bharadwaj, Vijay Madhav Joshi and Wishnu Mitter Sodhi. The Vampires were met by PAF's Sqn Ldr Sarfaraz Ahmed Rafiqui and his wingman Flt Lt Imtiaz Bhatti. The vastly superior Sabres went after the leading two Vampires who, instead of breaking off and escaping, tried to get behind the Sabres to fight it out. In the dogfight that followed, the two leading Vampires were shot down by Rafiqui, and Bhatti shot down the third. Bhagwagar, Bharadwar and Joshi did not stand a chance. Although Sodhi was engaged by Bhatti, he managed to dive low and escape. The Sabres, now low on fuel, exited the scene. Completely oblivious of what had transpired, the third wave of Vampires entered the scene and shot up three of our own AMX tanks and blew up the trucks carrying vital ammunition for our beleaguered armoured squadron.

PAF Sabre jets attacking IAF Vampires over Chhamb

It needs to be remembered that the Vampire was an obsolete fighter. It had entered operational service in 1948. I, as a young eleven-year-old schoolboy, had seen them flying over Bombay Harbour in 1948. By 1965, they were hopelessly out of date and just no match for the American F-86 Sabre. The Vampire had a fuselage made of plywood with no ejection system. In short, it was a death trap and yet it was used against Pakistan during this war. Realizing, late in the day, that the Vampires were 'sitting ducks' for any fighter aircraft at that time, the IAF now sent Mysteres to take on the Pakistani assault.

Twenty-seven years later, Air Vice Marshal C.S. Doraiswamy, who followed up with raids by Mysteres, says, 'We had very sketchy information. We were told that the Pakistanis had completely overrun the area between Jaurian and Akhnur, so we hit everything we saw.'[18]

By this time, Alpha Squadron, 20 Lancers led by Maj. Shankar Roychowdhury (promoted later as Army Chief) managed to reach the scene. Bhaskar Roy was down to three tanks from fourteen, and Roychowdhury saw Bhaskar's upturned tank smouldering. Convinced that Bhaskar had been finished, he and his crew searched for bodies. He then saw those familiar, heavy-rimmed glasses peer from over the other side of the tank and a hoarse voice say, quite peeved, 'Chow, what took you so long? I need a ride, and do you have any bloody cigarettes?' Charlie Squadron, 20 Lancers had by then, on that fateful day, destroyed or disabled more than fifteen Pattons despite the fact that the AMX-13 tanks were no match for the Pattons.[19]

In accordance with the plan of Maj. Gen. Akhtar Hussain Malik, GOC Pakistani 12 Infantry Division, the capture of Akhnur Bridge which spanned the Chenab was to have been done by 1200 hours of 1 September. Due to the resistance and resilience of the troops of 191 Infantry Brigade, the Pakistanis were still on the other side of the Munawar Tawi at 1200 hours on 1 September but in accordance with the earlier plan, the PAF commenced attacking the bridge at 1200 hours. They were kept at bay by our anti-aircraft guns. 6 Rajput had by this time been placed at the Akhnur Bridge for its protection.

Pakistan fails to capitalize on its gains

Strangely, the anticipated thrust for the capture of Akhnur did not materialize that day. If the Pakistanis had maintained the momentum of their offensive, it would have created a major problem for the Indian defenders, because although troops had moved to the defence line at Kalit–Troti–Jaurian, they had not had time to prepare their defensive positions.

Having launched their offensive with such ferocity, it is inexplicable why the Pakistanis did not follow up their initial progress beyond the Munawar Tawi. Although, this has been commented upon in the Synopsis, it needs repetition here as it is relevant to this part of the battle.

Whereas it had been planned that 7 Pakistani Infantry Division would lead the advance in Phase 3 of Operation Grand Slam after the capture of Akhnur, for some unknown reason it was decided that the change of command would take place when their forces reached Jaurian. Maj. Gen. Akhtar Hussain Malik was now made to hand over command and control of Operation Grand Slam to Maj. Gen. Yahya Khan, GOC 7 Pakistani Infantry Division.

Rumours from Pakistan suggest that Ayub Khan, a Pathan, wanted to give the honour of capturing Akhnur to Maj. Gen. Yahya Khan, rather than to Maj. Gen. Akhtar Hussain Malik, an Ahmadiyya. Another rumour was that Ayub Khan did not want Malik to get too much honour and wanted to cut him down to size!

The defence of Akhnur

Irrespective of the reasons for the change in command of Operation Grand Slam, the fact is that Yahya Khan decided to postpone the offensive on 2 September and failed to capitalize on the gains that had accrued that far. Perhaps he wanted to consolidate or wanted to be briefed in some more detail about further operations.

Be that as it may, it allowed the Indians the time and opportunity to move 41 Indian Infantry Brigade to hold the Pakistanis on the hastily prepared defence line Kalit–Troti Heights–Jaurian and to move the remnants of 191 Infantry Brigade for the close defence of Akhnur. In addition, XV Corps ordered 28 Infantry Brigade, supported by 20 Lancers less two squadrons, to take up a delaying position on the Fatwal Ridge, 6 miles from Akhnur, by the morning of 4 September.

Pakistan resumed its offensive on the night of 3-4 September after a delay of forty-eight hours, but they could make no headway against the defences of 41 Infantry Brigade. On the morning of 4 September, Pakistan launched a full-fledged attack with 6 Frontier Force and 13 Lancers on the Troti Heights defences but the Indians defended resolutely, and the attack had to be called off. But this hasty defensive position without anti-tank mines could not withstand a concentrated offensive by a division-plus, and 41 Infantry Brigade were ordered to move to consolidate the defences at Akhnur on 5 September.

These defensive positions slowed down the Pakistani offensive and by 6 September, Pakistan's 10 Infantry Brigade and 102 Infantry Brigade Group had made very marginal gains. It was, however, considered too risky to allow the Pakistani offensive to make further progress towards Akhnur, and on 6 September, Indian Prime Minister Lal Bahadur Shastri took the momentous decision to open the second front in Punjab. This decision shocked Ayub Khan and GHQ Pakistan as they expected India to restrict the war to J & K, despite the Indian Prime Minister's warning that if attacked in J & K, India would choose to respond at a time and place of her own choosing.

In Pakistan, the reaction to the opening of the second front and India's offensive across the international border (IB) was one of panic. President Ayub Khan was visibly shaken at the sudden escalation of hostilities. In a meeting with the military staff, Nur Khan, the Chief of Air Staff of the PAF proposed implementing contingency plans that included raids on IAF airbases. Ayub Khan gave his assent to Nur Khan. With this, the initiative of attacking airbases of the rival air forces passed from the IAF to the PAF.

Opening of the second front

Opening of the second front implied that it was now an all-out war. Lahore and Sialkot were now under threat. GHQ Pakistan immediately ordered withdrawal of 4 Corps Artillery and 11 Cavalry from the Chhamb Sector and the threat to Akhnur was removed. The Indians now moved from defence to offence by attacking the Pakistani positions at Troti Heights and the Chhamb and Mandiala crossings. By 7 September, Pakistan's GHQ ordered the withdrawal of 10 Pakistani Infantry Brigade and the Indians continued attacking the Pakistani positions at Jaurian and the Chhamb and Mandiala crossings on the night of 9–10 September and day of 10 September, but made no appreciable headway.

Without doubt, it was the difficult decision taken by Prime Minister Lal Bahadur Shastri at a critical time of the war that turned the tide in this momentous battle.

On 10 September, 41 Indian Infantry Brigade was pulled out of Akhnur and moved to XI Corps.

The ground situation would remain unchanged till the ceasefire on 23 September 1965.

The air situation however radically changed after 2 September. That, however, is another story.

Postscript

1. In order to plan offensive, counter-offensive or defensive operations, sound intelligence is of paramount importance. Intelligence has been an Indian weakness that needs to be set right.
2. The area of Chhamb has been a battleground in most of the wars fought by India, but we did not seem, at that time, to accept its strategic importance. Without doubt, it will once again be an area of decision in the next war. It is important that we plan to make this battleground a death trap for the next Pakistani misadventure but the battle will have to be fought differently!
3. Unfortunately, we only react to the enemy. This has happened in all the wars we have fought: 1947–48, 1962, 1965 and 1999. The only time we have fought on our own terms was the 1971 Indo–Pak war, the reasons for which are well known.
4. Chhamb, Poonch and Kargil have been the common denominators in the wars we have fought in Jammu and Kashmir against Pakistan. These strategic battlegrounds will always be part of the Pakistani mindset. This needs to be considered as part of our 'thinking' for the future.

5. The Chhamb battleground is an ideal opportunity for 'jointness' within the Army itself—infantry, armoured corps and artillery. And, of course, between the Army and the Air Force.
6. During my command of 10 Infantry Division, I used to invite the pilots of the fighter squadrons in support of the Chhamb operations for a briefing on the ground, so that they could have a clear idea of the physical features of the ground and what they could expect to see at each stage of the battle. Army–Air cooperation needs to be taken to the highest level to ensure victory in war.

6

The Avengers

'In war it is not always possible to have everything go exactly as one likes.'

—Winston Churchill

1 September 1965, 0600 hours

Brigadier Manmohan Singh, newly appointed commander of India's 191 Infantry Brigade, stared unbelievingly at the mass of Pakistani Patton tanks that were advancing ominously against the defences of his beleaguered brigade.

He had been desperately trying to convince Headquarters XV Corps that a huge Pakistani force of armour and infantry had assembled forward of his defences, but the Corps refused to believe him.[1] Now, this formidable adversary had appeared in front of him in no uncertain terms.

Pakistan had, in fact, launched its gigantic offensive, code-named Operation Grand Slam, early on the morning of 1 September 1965, with a devastating artillery barrage from 110 guns at 0330 hours. Now, after an overwhelming punishment lasting two and a half hours, the Pakistani armoured juggernaut of ninety tanks commenced its menacing advance, crushing everything that came in its path. The curtain of dust from the artillery barrage and the cacophony of sound from so many tanks made it difficult for the brigadier to see or hear anything else. The armoured thrust came from across the international border (IB) rather than from across the CFL, both of which were ahead of his brigade.

Notwithstanding the overwhelming force that faced them, the infantry soldiers of 3 Mahar and 6 Sikh LI put up a fierce resistance. They ducked into their trenches as the tanks passed overhead and resurfaced and took on the Pakistani infantry that was following in the wake of the tanks. Their infantry RCLs and the AMX tanks of 20 Lancers took on the advancing Pakistani Pattons and before they knew what hit them, twenty Pakistani Pattons had been destroyed or disabled.

1 September, 1100 hours

Brig. Manmohan Singh was, however, aware that there were limits to the resistance that his troops could put up against this overwhelming force and that he needed to do something worthwhile to stop this juggernaut in its tracks. It was now close to 1100 hours on 1 September.

Major General Akhtar Hussain Malik, GOC of Pakistan's 12 Infantry Division, had planned to reach Akhnur, just 20 miles from the border, by 1200 hours on

Day 1 of the offensive, but his advance was still stuck west of the Munawar Tawi, thanks to the staunch resistance of the troops of 191 Infantry Brigade.

Although Pakistan and India were at war, the conflict was restricted to Jammu and Kashmir, and their respective air forces had not yet entered the fray. In view of the criticality of the situation, Brig. Manmohan Singh decided to ask for air support. The use of air meant enlarging the war and permission from the Government of India was needed. The Army Chief, General Chaudhuri, was away from Army Headquarters, but he was informed of the seriousness of the situation in Chhamb and on his return to Delhi, he met Air Chief Marshal Arjan Singh and together went to the office of the Raksha Mantri, Shri Yashwantrao Chavan. The sanction of the Prime Minister and the Emergency Coordinating Committee (ECC) was also necessary for air power to be used, but the Raksha Mantri, being aware that time was of the essence, gave his go-ahead. It was now around 1700 hours—nearly five hours after the request by Brig. Manmohan Singh was made for air support!

1 September, 0430 hours, Pathankot

Prior to the Army Chief's arrival in Delhi, he had visited Pathankot and had alerted the airbase there about the developments in Chhamb. Being the nearest airbase to Chhamb, the fly-in would take just a few minutes.

Sqn Ldr S.K. Dahar, an enthusiastic and energetic commanding officer of 45 Squadron kept his squadron of

Vampires ready in anticipation of orders from the Chief of Air Staff. He planned to fly three missions: the first at 1719 hours, the second at 1730 hours and the third at 1740 hours. Sqn Ldr Dahar would lead the first mission. After a few adjustments, Flt Lt Bhagwagar was tasked to lead the second mission and Flt Lt F.J. Mehta, the third. The third mission would arrive over the battlefield at dusk, just as darkness was setting in and would return in fading light. Therefore, the pilots needed to be night-flying qualified.

The Vampire was the most obsolete aircraft in the Indian Air Force inventory at that time. Its first flight was during World War II. As a young boy of eleven years, I saw them flying over Bombay Harbour in 1948! At that time, even the propeller-driven Tempest had a higher rate of climb than the Vampire. In 1965, it was hopelessly out of date! Portions of the fuselage were made of wood and it lacked an ejection seat! The pilots of the third wave kept flashlights in their pockets to help them read the poorly lit instrument panels.[2]

At around 1700 hours, 1 September, HQ 191 Infantry Brigade received intimation that their request for air support had been processed and anxious eyes scanned the skies. At around 1720 hours, all eyes were turned upward at the sound of approaching aircraft and the appearance of the Vampires was greeted with great relief. Their joy, however, turned to horror as the Vampires, instead of attacking the Pakistani Pattons and gun positions, attacked their own defensive positions.

Having wreaked sufficient damage, they then turned their attention to the Pakistanis. No sooner had they done so when one of the Vampires was struck by Pakistani ground fire and crashed to the ground. The pilot, Flt Lt S.V. Pathak, was able to bail out from his stricken aircraft.

As soon as this happened, the Pakistan Army called for support from the Pakistan Air Force (PAF), and two F-86 Sabres armed with Sidewinder missiles entered the battle zone just as the second wave of Vampires led by Flt Lt Bhagwagar made its appearance. The Sabres were piloted by Sqn Ldr Sarfaraz Ahmed Rafiqui and Flt Lt Imtiaz Bhatti.

The obsolete Vampires were 'sitting ducks' for the far superior Sabres and the ground troops were extremely dismayed to see three out of the four Vampires shot out of the sky—only one managed to escape by diving down and flying at treetop level. In their outdated aircraft, the gallant Indian Air Force pilots paid the price for choosing to fight the far superior F-86 Sabres. Having destroyed four Vampires in this unequal air battle, the Sabres exited the battlefield.

At Pathankot, the ground crew waited anxiously for the return of the Vampires and they were extremely disappointed and disillusioned to learn that four of the Vampires were missing.

The Vampires were followed by four waves of Mysteres who continued to attack the Indian positions. They claimed thirteen tanks, two guns and sixty-two soft-vehicles destroyed but the ground troops stated that the tanks claimed as destroyed were three of our own AMX tanks of 20 Lancers and tanks that had already been destroyed by our ground troops. Twelve of our vehicles carrying valuable artillery and tank ammunition required for the ground battle were also destroyed by our own aircraft.

It is difficult to fathom why the sub-standard Vampires were sent in the first wave when the Mysteres were available. Although the Mysteres were also no match for the Sabres, they were certainly of a higher calibre than the Vampires. The possible reasons for using the Vampires in the first instance are as follows:

a. The IAF higher command perhaps felt that the PAF would not intervene at this stage, as all-out war had not yet been declared.
b. The Vampires were sent in first because they could not be used at a later stage that day, as they did not have night-flying capability.
c. The over-eagerness of the Vampire squadron commander who wanted to get into battle without taking into consideration the limitations of the Vampires.

The reasons for the damage caused by the IAF against our own troops was primarily poor briefing on the battle situation and the position of our battlefield locations and emplacements.

Flt Lt C.S. Doraiswamy (later AVM), who was part of the second wave of Mysteres, would ruefully say twenty-seven years later: 'We had very sketchy information. We were told that the Pakistanis had overrun the entire area between Jaurian and Akhnur, so we were hitting everything we saw. Amidst the glow from burning tanks, we had milliseconds to search for additional targets.'[3]

Brig. Manmohan Singh was disappointed that he had asked for air support. Not only had he suffered destruction and loss in terms of tanks and ammunition vehicles destroyed for whatever reason, it had also resulted in the loss of four Vampires of the IAF.

The Adventure of Flight Lieutenant S.V. Pathak

The reader would recall that Flt Lt S.V. Pathak, the Vampire pilot, who was shot down by Pakistani ground fire over Chhamb managed to bail out from his stricken aircraft. This was no mean feat, as the Vampire had no ejection system and Pathak had to turn his aircraft upside down, so as to fall out of the cockpit along with the parachute strapped to his back. On landing, he was not clear whether he was in Indian or Pakistani territory. He got rid of his parachute by hiding it in some trees and also his map and other papers that he had with him. Around this time, he noticed some police personnel with shoulder titles marked 'PP' chasing after the parachute and presumed that these were the Pakistani Police. So, he hid from them and headed due east, in which direction lay India and safety. After sometime, he entered a heavily forested area where he took shelter for the night and the next day, after which he once again started marching when the moon was up by moving from the shadow of one tree to another. Unknown to him, there was an army post in the area and in the dark, he stumbled over some sleeping soldiers who woke up totally startled. The soldiers raised an alarm and Pathak was immediately apprehended, handcuffed and blindfolded. One of the soldiers frisked Pathak and yelled '*Cartoos!*' when he found something that looked like a bullet, which was, in fact, the stub of a pencil. He was manhandled and one of the soldiers wounded him with a bayonet. Things would have got worse, and one of the soldiers wanted to finish him off, but for the intervention of a JCO. The JCO ordered the soldiers to take him to their officer.

The officer interrogated Pathak, but Pathak revealed only his name and number. Although initially, Pathak felt that he had been captured by Pakistani soldiers, from the talk of the soldiers he felt that perhaps he was in the hands of Indians. He now revealed that he was an Indian pilot who was flying a Vampire aircraft when he was shot down. On the contrary, the army officer who was interrogating Pathak felt that he was a Pakistani pilot and that he was lying because there were no Vampires at Pathankot. (The army officer did not know that the Vampires had flown in only a few days earlier.)

The officer informed his higher headquarters about Pathak's capture and after about two hours, they confirmed that a Vampire had been shot down and that Pathak was missing. The officer apologized to Pathak and dispatched him to Jammu in a Jeep along with two soldiers to look after him. Pathak was thereafter taken to Air Force Station Pathankot and flown from there to the Military Hospital, Delhi.

It was at this stage that Air Headquarters took a decision to beef up IAF fighter defence forces with Gnat fighters.[4]

23 Squadron, which had Gnat fighters, were now ordered to move to Pathankot. The Gnats flew at very low level to avoid radar detection. Consequently, the PAF was ignorant of the move of the Gnat squadron to Pathankot. On arrival at Pathankot, they were briefed by the operations-in-charge. The briefing was curt and plain: 'We want you to shoot down the Sabres. How you do it is your problem, but the Sabres will have to be tackled.' The Gnats would have to take off at dawn, with a Mystere formation flying at medium altitude to lure out the Sabres. The Gnats would avoid radar detection by flying at a low level. Once the Amritsar Surveillance Unit (SU) reported the incoming PAF fighters, the Gnats would climb to engage the Pak interceptors. It would be a classic baiting mission; it was designed to inflict losses on the PAF and to make the point that the IAF could engage with the Sabres.[5]

3 September, 0300 hours

The Gnat pilots were woken up at 0300 hours on the morning of 3 September for the meteorological briefing, after which they walked to the dispersal area and checked their aircraft.

At 0700 hours, four Mysteres took off from Pathankot and set course for Chhamb. The Mysteres were flying at 1500 feet followed by the Gnats flying at 300 feet. The Mysteres and Gnats flew north towards Chhamb and using the Akhnur Bridge as a prominent landmark, turned left and headed for Chhamb.

Pakistani radar, which covered this airspace, tracked the Mysteres and warned a Pakistani combat air patrol

(CAP) of Sabres and Starfighters of the presence of the Indian fighter aircraft and directed them to intercept the intruders. Pakistani radar had not been able to track the four Gnats flying low and trailing behind the Mysteres.

The four Gnat pilots in the forward detachment were Sqn Ldr Johnny Greene with Murdeshwar as his wingman. Sikand and Pathania were the other two pilots. Following them was the section led by Trevor Keelor at 100 feet above ground level with Krishnaswamy as his wingman and Sandhu and Gill as the other two pilots. An eight-Gnat formation was a unique formation. While heading for Chhamb, the pilots could hear the calm voice of Sqn Ldr Dandapani on the radio as he relayed the information from 230 SU warning them of the incoming PAF fighter aircraft.

As soon as the Mysteres approached the Chhamb battle zone, they veered off to the right and exited the area. Once they disappeared, Johnny Greene and Murdeshwar pulled up to 3000 feet with Keelor's section covering their flanks.

It was Keelor who first spotted a Sabre diving down from 5000 feet to get behind Johnny Greene's section. Green was taking his section in a turn and the Sabre tried to put himself behind Murdeshwar. Pathania called out a warning and Greene, now aware of what was happening, turned his section steeply to port.

Keelor, in the meantime, moved his section behind the Sabre. He had to use his air brakes to lose speed and to pull a tighter turn to stay behind the Sabre. Keelor found the Sabre was dead ahead and now sandwiched between Greene's section and Keelor's Gnat.

Tiny Gnat chasing a PAF Sabre jet over Chhamb

Keelor opened fire with his 30 mm cannon from a distance of about 450 yards. The Sabre's right wing disintegrated and it flicked over into an uncontrollable dive.

The IAF claimed its first Sabre kill and Trevor Keelor became the first pilot to claim a jet air-to-air combat kill. It was the first time that the Gnat, which had not been tested in combat, claimed its first victim.

The shooting down of the Sabre destroyed the alleged invincibility of the F-86 Sabre. It was also a retribution for the Vampires downed over this same battlefield, and morale at the Pathankot airbase moved sky-high. The good news was communicated to the CAS Air Marshal Arjan Singh and the Raksha Mantri. The next day, the newspapers exulted in the news of a Sabre being destroyed by a Gnat.

4 September, 1515 hours

The next day, 4 September, a section of four Gnats took off for Chhamb. They were to meet up with a section of Mysteres over the Chhamb battleground. On arrival over Chhamb, they did not meet up with the Mysteres but saw four Sabres attacking Indian defences over Chhamb. The Gnats broke into the Sabres who were forced out of their attack pattern. Greene got behind the first Sabre but found himself too high in his angle of attack. He had to break away and the Sabre managed to escape. Meanwhile, Murdeshwar got behind another Sabre and found it dead centre in his sights. He pressed his firing button and after only one bullet from his 30 mm cannon, his gun jammed. One more Sabre was lucky to make its escape.

The third Sabre broke away and flew towards Akhnur. Pathania gave chase and fired 3-gun bursts. The Sabre started emitting smoke and crashed near Akhnur. Pathania reported that the pilot must have ejected. Pakistan later admitted that it had lost a Sabre flown by Flt Lt N.M. Butt who was rescued by a Pakistani helicopter, thus evading capture.

The Gnats returned to base with the satisfaction of another Sabre destroyed. Two Sabres were lucky to have got away, otherwise the total number of Sabres downed that day would have been four! The gun camera footage of Green and Murdeshwar showed the Sabres right in the centre of their gunsights.

For shooting down the Sabres, Keelor and Pathania were awarded the Vir Chakra as was Greene for leading them into combat.

The tiny Gnats had made their mark and proved they were more than a match for the Sabres, whose reputation of ascendancy was destroyed forever.

Destruction of a PAF Sabre jet by an IAF Gnat

Postscript

1. The Gnat was a small swept-wing light fighter aircraft made by Folland Aircraft, UK. With a wing-span of just 22 feet 1 inch, it was extremely difficult to spot a Gnat in the sky. Because of this, and its extreme agility in a dogfight, it was probably the best fighter aircraft for air combat against the US-made Pakistani F-86 Sabre jet.
2. Soon after the two Sabres were shot down by Denzil Keelor and Pathania, one more Sabre were shot down by Flt Lt Trevor Keelor flying a Gnat, making the Keelor Brothers a household name across India.
3. Subsequently, four more F-86 Sabres were destroyed, one each by Flying Officer Adi Gandhi

and Flt Lt D.N. Rathore and two by Flying Officer V.N. Neb in air combat, and one more by Flt Lt G.S. Thapa using a 20 mm aircraft gun in anti-aircraft mode, making a total of eight F-86 Sabres destroyed. Some of the air battles were recorded on gun cameras, making for dramatic coverage.

4. Two Sabres escaped due to gun stoppages of the Gnats, which goes to prove that luck does play a part in the individual destinies of soldiers in the arena of war. Napoleon Bonaparte, when considering a senior general for an important appointment, used to ask: 'Is he lucky?'

5. The shooting down of eight Pakistani F-86 Sabre jets was perhaps a fitting retribution for the four Vampires lost during the initial part of the war.

7

A Mission Fulfilled

'If you don't make mistakes, you are not really trying.'

—Coleman Hawk

This story is a sequel to the story 'It's Never Too Late' that is part of my book 'Beyond Fear'. The focus of that story was the courageous conduct of an Indian Air Force pilot of a sub-sonic Mystere who, on a raid on an enemy airfield at Sargoda, took on a supersonic Pakistani F-104 Starfighter and shot it down, at the expense of his own life. His act of valour was recognized twenty-three years after this incident due to the personal admission of the Pakistani pilot who described this encounter.

Although twelve Mysteres took off for Sargodha that morning, only six reached the target area. After he returned from the raid, the Squadron Commander, Wing Commander Om Taneja, carried out a review of why only six of his pilots reached the target area. He stated that the reasons given for failing to reach their objective were unacceptable. Most of his pilots were young. He felt that wrong lessons would be learnt by the pilots of his squadron, if corrective action was not taken. He therefore took a controversial but hard decision to send the section that had failed to reach the target area back to Sargodha. This time, in broad daylight, to ensure fulfilment of the Sargodha mission.

This is that story.

It was early morning of 7 September and twelve Mysteres of No. 1 Squadron—'The Tigers', were lined up in the dark on the Indian airfield at Adampur, preparatory to taking off for a raid on the Pakistani airfield at Sargodha.

The previous evening, a Pakistani B-57 bomber had dropped a bomb on the airfield and although it did no damage to the runway, it caused a great deal of earth to land at the periphery.

Due to a miscalculation by the planners, the time over target was given as 0555 hours and so the Tigers would be attacking their targets in the dark. Wing Commander Om Taneja asked for a change in time but his request could not be acceded to, because Hunters from Halwara would be attacking Sargodha again on termination of the raid by the Mysteres.

The squadron, led by Wing Commander Om Taneja, took off in pairs at thirty-second intervals, each aircraft occupying one half of the runway. To ensure secrecy, strict radio silence was maintained. Even the control tower kept quiet as the aircraft took off in pairs in the early morning darkness. The aircraft flew 300 feet above ground level to avoid being detected by Pakistani radar and the roar of the aircraft, so close to the ground, woke up sleepy villages on both sides of the border.

Sargodha was at the extreme range of the Mysteres, with a flight time of thirty minutes from Adampur. The entire operation was estimated to take one hour. Being on the outer limit of the Mysteres' range, no tactical rerouting was possible, nor could the aircraft be permitted the luxury of taking on additional targets. So, the aircraft could only hit targets on the Sargodha airfield and return. There was no time for anything else and the pilots were briefed accordingly.

The Mysteres returned to base around 0700 hours, and Wing Commander Taneja was waiting for Sqn Ldr 'Tubby' Devayya to join the debrief, but Tubby had not returned. Everyone was under the impression that Devayya was probably taking his time in the lines of 32 Squadron returning their borrowed aircraft. After a while, upon inquiring with 32 Squadron, it was found that Devayya had not returned. Taneja proceeded with the debrief of the mission.

During the debrief, it was learnt that two aircraft of the first wave aborted due to engine problems and the last section of four aircraft lost their way; initially due to the dust raised on the runway at take-off time due to the debris at the side, due to radio silence as well as the darkness and the fact that no one was allowed to use their navigation lights.

Wing Commander Taneja was unhappy with Squadron Commander Handa's section for failing to reach his target. He gave him a good dressing-down and ordered him to go back to Sargodha to finish his task along with his section.[1]

He clarified that India was at war with Pakistan and unless we hit them hard, we would be letting them off the hook. They had destroyed several aircraft on the ground at Pathankot and we needed to destroy their ability to fight. He added that considering the situation and the performance of this section, he had no option but to send them back to complete their unfinished mission. This was a most unexpected order because there would be no cover of darkness for the outbound leg and the alerted Pakistani defences would give them a hot reception. The chances of being intercepted by enemy fighters was also high. This time, the attack would be in broad daylight at 0945 hours.[2]

Meanwhile, with no information from anyone, Devayya was eventually listed as 'missing in action' and his whereabouts would remain a mystery for years to come.[3]

Handa's section consisted of himself in the lead, with 'Kay', Brar and Phillip Rajkumar as the remaining pilots of the section. After a quick breakfast, Sqn Ldr Handa went over the briefing once again to make sure there would be no errors this time. Since the attack would be in daylight, they were given specific targets from an aerial photograph taken some years earlier.

The plan was to carry out a shallow dive-bombing attack and release their bombs over their targets and pull out at about 200 feet above ground level (AGL). In order to avoid being damaged by the exploding bombs at such a low height, the bombs were fitted with 20-second delay fuses to give the aircraft adequate time to get clear. The return leg was to be flown at tactical speed as low a height as possible, consistent with safety.

The section took off exactly at 0945 hours in order to be over their targets at 1015 hours. It was a sunny and cloudless day with excellent visibility in low-level tactical formation. Handa was in front with Kay about 1000 yards to his right. Brar and Phillip Rajkumar were behind and to the outside of the leaders at a distance of about 200 yards.

In this way, Brar could look to his right and clear the areas behind Phillip Rajkumar to spot any approaching enemy fighters and Phillip could do the same for him by looking left. By this time, Handa had descended to 100 feet AGL.

As they crossed the international border, Brar fired a short gun-burst to check that his guns were firing properly and Phillip did the same. No enemy aircraft were visible.

The railway line to Sargodha was a landmark that became visible and Handa turned left to follow it to Sargodha. This was the moment to open to full power, turn on the armament switches and accelerate to full speed. Two minutes later, Handa called out that he was pulling up and all four aircraft eased up to 2500 feet and rolled on to a shallow dive. As they settled into their dive, they could see the Sargodha runway and their identified targets they were to destroy. The four aircraft were now strung out in a line, with Handa in front and Phillip about 1500 feet behind him at the top of the dive.

IAF Mysteres in formation on the approach to Sargodha

Suddenly, Handa yelled, 'Aircraft at the end of the runway!' After dropping his bombs on a bulk petroleum installation to the north of the runway, Handa spotted four enemy aircraft—three F-86 Sabres and one 10F-104 Starfighter parked on the Operational Readiness Platform (ORP) and went for them. He opened fire with his guns, blowing up a Sabre with his burst. Phillip yelled, 'Sir, you got him!' The anti-aircraft guns of Sargodha airfield now opened up and black puffs of smoke close to them indicated that they were the targets. Phillip Rajkumar dropped his bombs on his designated target and opened his guns on an aircraft on the southern ORP, but there was no explosion, indicating that it was probably a decoy.

After Handa had called out about the aircraft, Kay spotted them. Once Handa had pulled out of his dive, Kay opened up with a long burst of his 30 mm DFA cannons on the enemy aircraft on the ground. However, he could not make out whether he had hit the aircraft on the ORP.

The aircraft pulled out of their dive at barely 100 feet AGL. Handa's aircraft was now approximately 800 yards ahead, heading for base.

Handa now called out, 'Confirm all are with me.' All confirmed, 'All with you, Sir.' They were now flying in two pairs on a broad frontage with Handa and Brar in front and Kay and Phillip Rajkumar about 800 yards behind. The fighters were flying very low and their jet wake was cutting a swathe over the standing crops in the fields. While flying to the north of Lahore, Phillip called out, 'Bogey left

A Mission Fulfilled

7 o'clock high' and Handa called out 'Buster', which meant opening full power as they headed for home. Fuel levels of all four aircraft were low by this time and Phillip's red warning light came on, indicating a fuel reserve of just 10 minutes. While flying over Amritsar, our own anti-aircraft guns opened up on them. Fortunately, no one was hit. By this time, all four aircraft were within range of Adampur airfield and were able to land without mishap, although with very little fuel left in their tanks.

Handa's log book entries on his return to base state that he strafed three F-86 Sabres and one F-104 Starfighter, claiming at least one F-86 Sabre destroyed and two F-86 Sabres and one F-104 Starfighter as probables.[4]

IAF Mysteres attacking Sargodha airfield

Postscript

Although the decision by Wing Commander Om Taneja to send part of his squadron back to Sargodha to complete their unfinished task was fraught with high risk, fortune favours the brave. With one F-86 claimed as destroyed and three other enemy fighters claimed as probables, the mission was certainly a success.

8

Ambushed!

'The bend in the road is not the end in the road; unless you fail to take the turn.'

—Helen Keller

The debacle of the Sino-Indian war of 1962 forced the Government of India to acknowledge that the Indian armed forces had been neglected and that a major overhaul was needed to bring them back to the level of effectiveness that they had earlier enjoyed. It was accepted that the armed forces needed to be revamped, reorganized and equipped so that they could effectively carry out their duty to safeguard the nation. When *TIME* magazine reported on the Sino-Indian war of 1962, it declared, 'The Indian Army needs almost everything except courage.'

As a result of this realization, orders for the raising of more army units were given. One more battalion of the 5th Gorkha Rifles (FF) was ordered to be raised at our regimental centre at Dehradun, from 1 January 1963.

Actually, it was a re-raising, because the 4th Battalion the 5th Gorkha Rifles (FF) was raised during World War II and had distinguished itself in Burma. Being a war-raised unit and the junior-most battalion of the regiment at that time, it was disbanded after the conclusion of World War II. It was now being given an opportunity to distinguish itself once again.

Three officers from the 1st Battalion the 5th Gorkha Rifles (FF) were posted to the new battalion—the CO Col S.S. Jog, the adjutant Capt. J.S. Rawat and I. I was a junior captain then, with just about four and a half years' service. A number of JCOs, NCOs and other ranks were also posted to the battalion that had to be raised. Knowing how emotionally difficult it was for officers and men to leave what was considered home and family for life, the orders stated that the move had to take place within forty-eight hours and that no representation would be entertained. Officers and men from all battalions of the regiment were posted to make up the strength of the new fourth battalion.

We worked hard to get the battalion into shape and within six months, the battalion was declared 'fit for war'. It was moved to Jammu and Kashmir to hold picquets along the Cease-Fire Line (CFL). The Pakis usually get to know when a change of units is taking place along the CFL and use ingenious methods to test the new unit. Warned about this, we decided to give them a run for their money. Heavy firing from them was responded to by silence from us. They did not know what to make of it!

After a number of days of firing on their part, they decided to approach one of our picquets to check whether we were sleeping! We let them approach till they came close and then we opened fire. The message was not lost on them and they came to know we meant business.

Somewhere about the fourth week of November 1964, Pakistani saboteurs crossed the CFL and laid anti-personnel mines on a track leading to one of our picquets, and one of our soldiers was killed. A flag meeting was held, and we told them that this was a cowardly thing to do and they would pay for it. Predictably, they denied complicity. For the next one month, they were extraordinarily alert. We waited for about a month to let them relax a bit and then launched a raid across the CFL in what is today euphemistically called a 'surgical strike'. The raid was led by me and Maj. M.M.P. Kala. We caused sufficient damage to convey to them that such acts would not be tolerated. The weapons we captured were handed over to the brigade.

Around July 1965, the battalion had done two years on the CFL, but we never had the opportunity to do 'collective training' since the date we had been raised. We requested for permission to be withdrawn from the CFL to train. Permission was granted and we came down from our picquets and set up camp south of Rajouri in the first few days of August. It appeared, however, that our attempt to do 'collective training' was jinxed.

Pakistan's obsession to take J & K with force tempted her around the first week of August 1965 to replicate her earlier failed attempt of 1947–48.

Looking at the events that had transpired during those years, the political and military hierarchy of Pakistan apparently concluded that India had not yet been able to reorganize her forces after the Sino-Indian war of 1962.

Pakistan had received significant economic assistance and massive military aid from the US, amounting to more than $1.5 billion. The military aid included 400 Patton tanks, one squadron of supersonic F-104 Starfighters, four squadrons of F-86 Sabre jet fighters, two squadrons of B-57 bombers, artillery guns to equip medium and heavy artillery regiments, and sophisticated communication systems. This completely upset the balance of power and relative strength in the subcontinent.

At this time, General Ayub Khan, who had come to power through a military coup, felt that the opportunity was ripe to attempt once again to take Jammu and Kashmir from India by force. After the death of Pandit Nehru on 27 May 1964, he felt that India had lost its political will and that this was therefore the right time to strike, as such an opportunity was unlikely to arise again.

General Ayub consulted with his corps commanders and directed them to make military plans to execute his aim. Pakistan's military planners came up with a series of military offensives which they felt would achieve their aim of wresting Kashmir from India. These were Operation Desert Hawk, Operation Gibraltar and Operation Grand Slam.

Operation Desert Hawk, in the Rann of Kutch, aimed to take a measure of India's political and military leadership, to test Pakistan's ability to effectively handle the military equipment given to her by the US, and to lull India away from the issue of Jammu and Kashmir. As a follow-up of this operation, Pakistan planned to launch Operation Gibraltar, which involved the dispatch of a large force of guerrillas across the CFL to create anarchy in the hinterland of the state of J & K and to label it as a civil uprising. The third offensive was code-named 'Operation Grand Slam' whose aim was to sandwich Indian troops on the CFL between a division-sized force attacking from the front and guerrillas attacking from the rear.

Meanwhile, the battalion, unaware of what Pakistan was up to, pitched a tented camp at Sarol, south of Rajouri. The commanding officer, Lt Col Madan Bhatia, who had not had a break ever since he took command of the battalion, decided to go on leave. Maj. Prem Das, the second-in-command, took command of the unit as the Officiating CO.

We had just finished lunch after a training conference when we heard shots fired from one of our outlying picquets that were guarding our camp. This was followed by a heavy exchange of fire. On checking, we found that an infiltrating enemy guerrilla column had hit one of our posts and a number of guerrillas were killed, a few were taken prisoner and the remainder retreated.

Apparently, our battalion was one of the first units to encounter an infiltrating column that formed part of Pakistan's Operation Gibraltar. Interrogation of these captured guerrillas revealed that a large force of guerrillas organized into ten columns had crossed the CFL between Ladakh and Jammu. They also revealed that plans for Operation Gibraltar had been made in May 1965. Pakistan unsurprisingly denied all complicity and tried to pass it off as a civil uprising by the citizens of Jammu and Kashmir. However, clear evidence of Pakistan's involvement was reported by the UN Observer Group and mentioned as such by the UN Secretary General U Thant in the Security Council on 3 September 1965.[1] Further, it was also revealed that Gen. Ayub Khan had himself addressed the force commanders of Operation Gibraltar in the second week of July 1965 at Murree in Pakistan.

Further to the north, within the divisional sector, shepherds reported that a strange group of armed men had gathered in a forest close to our brigade headquarters. Capt. C.N. Singh, an officer from the Garhwal Rifles posted to the brigade headquarters, took a patrol to investigate and was ambushed and killed. The guerrilla force withdrew and moved away, probably to the vicinity of Bhimber Galli.

At this juncture, our battalion was the only one in the divisional sector that was not holding ground and so we willy-nilly became the divisional reserve.

My company, Alpha Company, was ordered to move to the brigade headquarters and we went post-haste. Subsequently, the rest of the battalion closed up to the brigade headquarters and established itself adjacently. A day after we had moved to the brigade headquarters, we were told that a group of guerrillas had established itself at Pir Kalewa. This was a high hill feature in the depth area of the division, and I recalled that our forces had fought a battle on this feature with the Pakistanis during the Indo–Pak war of 1947–48.

Alpha Company was tasked to deal with the guerrillas.

We left well before daybreak as Pir Kalewa was a long way off and a stiff climb was involved. The ridge line, of which Pir Kalewa was a part, was covered by dense forests of fir trees. We reached an adjoining knoll of the same ridge line that had a spectacular view of the whole of the Rajouri Sector. It was evident that Pir Kalewa was occupied because wisps of smoke were filtering through the trees. It appeared that the guerrillas were preparing their afternoon meal. Subedar Bhimbahadur and I were working out our plan to assault the feature when all of a sudden, artillery rounds crashed on to the feature. We could hear cries of alarm and the guerrillas left in a hurry, taking what they could with them. We learnt later on that it was Maj. Prem Das, the Officiating CO, who had organized the artillery fire on to the hill feature.

We rushed up the feature but the surprise element had been lost. The fires were still burning. We put them out to prevent a forest fire, carried out a search of the area and found articles of clothing and ammunition that were of no use to us. We then carried out a search of the next feature and the one beyond that, but the guerrillas had disappeared as they normally do in such situations. So, we decided to return to base.

After descending from the higher ridge line of the fir forests, we reached the pine tree line. Range upon range of pine-covered ridges extended into the distance as far as the eye could see. Suddenly, we saw two fighter planes attacking a feature that was hidden from us. We wondered whether these were ours or enemy aircraft and what they were firing at.

We reached the brigade headquarters after about six hours of hard marching and learnt to our consternation that it was our battalion that was the target of those Pakistani Sabre jets.

PAF Sabre jets attacking location of 4/5 GR (FF) at Galuthi

Apparently, an Army Service Corps (ASC) vehicle convoy seeing our battalion on the verge of the road stopped to take a break. Two Pakistani Sabre jets that were on the prowl saw this convoy and found it too lucrative a target to ignore. After using their cannons on their first circuit, they followed up with napalm bombs. Although the use of napalm bombs is banned by the Geneva Convention, such aspects mattered little to the Pakistani armed forces.

Napalm bombs create great walls of fire and burn to cinders anything and everything in their path. Unfortunately, Maj. Prem Das, who was trying to disperse the troops after the first attack, was caught in the fire wall of the bombs and was burnt to death. He was the first second-in-command of 'Four Five' to die. Seven more were to become casualties in the ensuing years, but that's another story.

Alpha Company, in addition to providing protection to the brigade headquarters, was tasked for convoy protection duties from Pathankot to Poonch. Being aware that the more threatened area was between Rajouri and Poonch, I detailed my company officer, 2/Lieutenant Dinesh Singh Rana, to take command of the convoy from Pathankot to Rajouri and I took on the area between Rajouri and Poonch.

Information had been received that convoys to Poonch had been ambushed by the guerrillas and the drivers had been tied to trees, bayoneted and set on fire. As a consequence, no convoys were able to reach Poonch and it remained cut off for about ten days.

Since I had been tasked to escort a large convoy of over 250 vehicles, and the threat was considerable, I visited the divisional headquarters to request for light vehicles (Jeeps) so that I could move my mortars and MMGs up and down the convoy to the point of decision in the event of being ambushed. The GSO1 (Ops) of the division, Lt Col Harish Bakshi, was from our regiment, and I felt that my request would be acceded to. Unfortunately, he was away, so I went with my request to the AQ (Ops). Instead of acceding to my request, I received a long lecture for making what he considered was an unreasonable demand and he sent me away saying he did not know what the army was coming to with officers like me. I was disappointed.

On my way out, I met Brigadier J.B.F. Fridell, the Commander Artillery, who asked me what I was doing at the division headquarters. I explained my need and that the AQ had turned down my request for Jeeps to move my mortars and MMGs. Being aware of the situation, he said, 'I will see what I can do to provide you with artillery cover. You will need a Forward Observation Officer (FOO) with a radio set to communicate with the guns. It's not a promise but I will try.'

Early next morning, I briefed the Army Supply Corps (ASC) JCO who was the convoy commander and the drivers. The ASC JCO was from Assam and came across as a person with a positive attitude. I was happy to have him with me. It was a long convoy of approximately 250 vehicles. We had to keep a distance of 25 metres between vehicles and that made the convoy over 5 km long. To protect the convoy, I had a platoon of less than thirty men. I briefed them on how they would be organized and the action to be taken in the event of being ambushed. I had a Jeep from my unit but no Jeeps for the mortars and MMGs. Instead, my mortars and MMGs were mounted on two Chevrolet trucks, which were called 'ulloo' trucks, probably because of the flat shape of their bonnets that gave them an 'owlish' look. They also had frequent breakdowns and were slower than the Dodge, which was perhaps another reason it was given this name.

We first had a 3-ton vehicle with a light machine gun (LMG) tied to the superstructure. The first section of the platoon was mounted on this vehicle along with my 2ic Subedar Bhimbahadur Rana. His JC number was JC-11111 and he was thus known in the battalion as 'Ek Saab'.

Subedar Bhimbahadur was very tough morally, mentally and physically. An excellent company 2ic, he was intense and passionate about his duties.

A platoon consists of three sections, each section having a strength of ten men. Since I had less than thirty men to protect such a long convoy, I placed one section in the leading 3-ton, one section in the middle of the convoy and the third section at the tail of the column. Subedar Bhimbahadur was in the leading vehicle sitting next to the driver and I was in the middle of the convoy with the mortar and MMG detachments close behind me in their 'ulloo' trucks.

The road from Rajouri goes through a pass at Bhimber Galli. The road from Bhimber Galli to Poonch runs for 55 km along a ridge which is about 1000 feet high. The ridge was covered with clumps of pine trees interspersed with maize plantations and walnut trees, and had a gradient of about thirty to forty degrees.

On our way to Poonch, a few kilometres beyond Bhimber Galli, we came across about twenty to thirty guerrillas digging up the road. They were trying to create a roadblock. There were masses of them concentrated in groups along the ridge. We dispersed those who were on the road with a few bursts from an LMG and followed with some more bursts as they clambered up the ridge.

I now realized that I could have created havoc with these guerrillas had I got the artillery support that the Commander Artillery had said he would try to give me.

Meanwhile, Subedar Bhimbahadur had collected the leading section with the aim of chasing the guerrillas and eliminating them. I explained to him that our primary task was to take the convoy to Poonch as quickly as possible, and a stalled convoy spread over a distance of over 6 km would be an excellent target for the hundreds of guerrillas sitting on the ridge. He reluctantly agreed and we proceeded to Poonch without further incident. At Poonch, we were received like heroes. We had no idea that the situation was that bad.

Meanwhile, I told the ASC JCO to coordinate with the brigade headquarters staff to have the vehicles unloaded and sent the next day for maintenance because I did not want any breakdowns on my way back.

I had just finished briefing the convoy commander and my company 2ic, when I received a message that the Brigade Commander wanted to see me. After congratulating me for bringing the convoy safely into Poonch, he told me that there were another 200 vehicles stranded at Poonch and he wanted those vehicles and mine to move out of Poonch the next day.

He added that there was not enough place to park so many vehicles in the Poonch garrison, the only other area being the airfield, which was under observation and shelling from enemy guns. It was therefore essential that all these vehicles left Poonch as early as possible.

I informed the Brigade Commander that I had broken an ambush in the vicinity of Bhimber Galli on my way up to Poonch and had seen approximately 200 to 300 guerrillas on the ridge above the road. I was certain that they would be waiting for the return of the convoy the next day. It would not be possible for me with just thirty men to protect a convoy of about 450 vehicles, which would extend to a column of about 10 km—we would be sitting ducks for the guerrillas and a lucrative target.

The Brigade Commander was now beginning to get irritated. He said, 'This is war and I am giving you an order. Do it, or face the consequences.'

'Sir, I do not come under your command. I come directly under the Division Commander. I suggest you speak with him before insisting that I take the convoy back tomorrow,' I shot back.

The Brigade Commander got very angry but he knew what I had said was correct. He rang the division and asked to speak with the GOC. After listening to the Brigade Commander's complaint, the GOC asked, 'Have you asked Major Cardozo as to what he needs to carry out your orders?'

'No sir,' said the Brigade Commander.

'Ask him,' said the GOC.

The Brigade Commander glared at me and asked, 'What do you want?'

I said, 'Two rifle companies to protect the convoy or have the ridge above the road from Kalai Bridge to Bhimber Galli held halfway by your brigade and halfway by my brigade and I will take the convoy through.'

'Why did you not say so in the first place?'

'Because you did not ask me and because the drivers need rest and time to maintain their vehicles.'

'All right. The ridge line will be held. Plan to leave tomorrow morning by 9.30 and that's an order.'

'Okay sir. However, the drivers would not have had enough sleep and the vehicles would not have been maintained.'

The Brigade Commander did not say anything and I left. Fortunately, the ASC JCO and Subedar Bhimbahadur were awake and I was able to brief them about what was to be done the next morning.

The next day at 8 a.m., I got all the drivers together and briefed them as to what I expected of them in the event of an ambush. Basically, all that was required of them was to proceed at a steady speed, keeping the inter-vehicle distance of 25 metres, and to keep to the left of the road giving me space to move my mortars and MMGs up and down the convoy. I thereafter briefed Subedar Bhimbahadur, the ASC JCO and my platoon separately.

As directed by the Brigade Commander, the convoy moved out of Poonch exactly at 9.30 a.m. Three busloads of civilians had also been added to the convoy. This was not part of my assignment but I accepted it as a part of the exigencies of war and placed them at the tail end of the convoy.

I waited at Kalai Bridge, which was the starting point, until the last vehicle left and started moving up the road checking that I had enough space to move my 'ulloo' trucks.

After about an hour and a half, when I had reached somewhere near the middle of the convoy, I heard a loud explosion and the chattering of machine guns. I raced forward in my jeep. I was accompanied by my runner Girbahadur, a curly-haired young soldier and my driver. For my weapon, I carried a Mk 4 rifle. It was a .303 rifle with a smaller stock and lighter than the unwieldy .303 Mk 3 rifle. I never carried a Sten machine carbine because it had a history of stoppages.

Ambushed!

When we reached the initial part of the ambush site, Girbahadur and I climbed up the embankment and saw in front of us, a whole line of guerrillas firing on to the convoy. With my rifle, I fired at an LMG group closest to us—hardly 50 feet away! I dropped the Pakistani soldier manning the LMG, reloaded and fired at the second Pakistani soldier, when a Pakistani NCO saw us and started shouting, *'Kafir ka major—zinda pakro! Zinda pakro!* (An enemy (unbeliever) major! Catch him alive!)'

There was no point in fighting them. I could have shot the Pakistani NCO who was advancing towards me but this was no time for heroics. Getting into a firefight with just Girbahadur and me against this whole horde of guerrillas would be pointless. My responsibility was the convoy and my task was its protection. The convoy had come to a halt and I had to get to the mortars and MMGs to get us out of this situation. So, Girbahadur and I jumped down from the embankment and ran down the road looking for the 'ulloo' trucks.

After about 800 metres, I found the truck carrying the mortars—but the mortars and the mortar crew was missing! 'Tekbahadur!' I yelled, wondering what had happened to the mortar detachment commander with the full realization that without the mortars, the situation would be impossible. I was relieved to hear him answer: *'Yahan chha, Saab! Mo ayo* (I am here Saab, I am coming).'

'Where are you and what are you doing?' I shouted.

'I have climbed to the top of this ridge and I can see the ambush site and have laid the mortars accordingly.'

'Why have you not started firing?' I asked.

'I don't know where our boys are,' he said in Nepali.

I ordered him to open fire. Tekbahadur opened fire with his mortars and at the same time I saw Havildar Karnabahadur with the middle section on the skyline hurrying towards the ambush site.

I told Tekbahadur to keep locating the enemy and firing at them, and I joined Karnabahadur and his section on top of the ridge.

They were firing at the guerrillas who had moved en masse to the reverse slope of the ridge due to the mortar fire. We could see the Pakistani JCOs and NCOs beating the guerrillas with *lathis* (sticks) in an effort to get them back to the top of the ridge.

Ambush between Poonch and Bhimber Galli, 21 August 1965

I made Karnabahadur keep shifting his LMG to make the Pakistanis think that we were a platoon and not just a section. Meanwhile, Tekbahadur had managed to drop a few mortar bombs where the guerrillas had gathered. This was too much for them. They scattered and the Pakistani JCOs and NCOs could not get them back.

I ran down the ridge to the convoy and saw that some ASC drivers had been killed and some had been wounded. Luckily, I came across a Gorkha Naik from 11 Gorkha Rifles who was on deputation to the Corps of Military Police. He was going on leave. I told him to get 'second drivers' and, if necessary, civilians from the buses who could drive heavy vehicles, to drive the driverless trucks and get the convoy moving, as I wanted them out of this area before last light. He managed to do what I had said, and after I saw that the convoy had started to move, I hurried towards the front to see how Bhimbahadur and the first section had fared.

What I saw devastated me. Subedar Bhimbahadur was dead. He had decapitated the Pakistani soldier who had fired a rocket at the convoy and his khukri was buried in the head of the number 2 of the guerrilla rocket launcher team. His body was riddled with bullets, but he had a peaceful smile on his face as if he had finally achieved what he wanted to all along.

The scene at the leading 3-ton was gruesome. The tailboard was down and the floorboard was awash with congealed blood. The rocket fired by the Pakistanis had taken off the heads of Naik Dilijang Gurung and one more soldier, and what remained of their bodies lay in a heap on the floor of the truck. Four others who had continued to man the LMG were badly wounded and were being evacuated.

By now, my CO had arrived from the brigade headquarters with two companies. The battalion had apparently received a message from the Poonch brigade that they should move and hold part of the ridge line but there was no transport and they had to move on foot. They arrived too late.

By this time, I was furious. It had become clear that I was wrongly informed that I could move the convoy when the ridge line had, in fact, not been held. It became clear to me that the Poonch brigade had not held their part of the ridge. This was confirmed by Havildar Karnabahadur, that he had not seen anyone from the Poonch brigade during his move from their part of the sector, and in our part of the sector, there were only Pakistani guerrillas.

Meanwhile the convoy began moving on its way to Rajouri and beyond. I was busy at the Brigade Transport Checking Point evacuating the wounded, when I received a phone call from the BM, Maj. 'Tiger' Thyagraja, that the Brigade Commander wished to speak with me. I am afraid I was rude and told the BM that I was busy evacuating the wounded and if the Brigade Commander wished to speak with me, he could come up to where I was, and that in any case I was going to ask for a Court of Inquiry as to why this had happened. The Brigade Commander complained to my CO that I was being rude and impertinent, and I received a 'shut up call' from my CO.

I was miserable and restless and did not know what to do. I had lost my company 2ic, my best NCOs and men, all because I had worked on trust. The next few days were spent cremating the dead and the follow-up action that is required to fill in the requisite documents for those who had been killed. My strength needed to be made up, but all the companies were below strength and all that I got was Naib Subedar Prem Singh, the newly promoted Military Transport (MT) Havildar to fill in the vacancy caused by the death of Subedar Bhimbahadur Rana.

Gorkhas are cheerful, stoic in times of distress and always with a positive attitude. I realized that I should not pass on my discomfort to the rest of my company and so, after a brief period when I reorganized my sections and platoons, I organized a basketball match and joined my men for their evening meal in the *langar* (cook house) where we talked about what we should do to be ready for the next operation. Little did I realize that it would happen very soon.

Postscript

Although in the army, one works on trust, I learnt that it is important to check and double-check on assurances given by various agencies. Without a doubt, at times, even after checking, it would be necessary to carry out an operation without the promised facilities but that would be on the basis of calculated risks. Success in operations depends on the will and determination of the leader and the troops that he leads.

9

Jumbahadur

Bravery, Loyalty, Gaiety—the hallmark of soldiers of the 5th Gorkha Rifles (FF)

Jumbahadur and I joined the regiment about the same time; Jumbahadur as a rifleman from the 58 Gorkha Training Centre and I as a 2/Lieutenant, newly commissioned from the Indian Military Academy. Both institutions were located at Dehradun but we first set eyes on each other only when we joined the 1st Battalion the 5th Gorkha Rifles (FF). This was the battalion in which Jumbahadur's father and many men from his village were still serving. Little did either of us realize that our lives and destinies would be closely linked in the years to come. It was a tradition in the regiment to recruit successive generations of soldiers from the same family. The 1st Battalion the 5th Gorkha Rifles (FF) had many soldiers of the fifth generation serving in it. Jumbahadur therefore had the prerogative to join his father's battalion.

I was appointed Company Officer in Alpha Company. Jumbahadur was a rifleman in a different company. Jumbahadur and I, however, found ourselves doing the same basic training for riflemen and undergoing the same routine for soldiers. It was a custom of the battalion that all officers in their first month of service underwent the same training and routine as the soldiers. In this way, we were able to understand exactly what the men went through and the high standards that were demanded of them.

Jumbahadur was younger than me by about two years. He was short but what he lacked in height, he made up in enthusiasm. He was lively, energetic and willing to try his hand at anything. Most important was his attitude. He was always happy and cheerful. He was never discouraged by any setback and his shining eyes reflected his positive outlook on life.

A few years after we joined the battalion, India went to war with China and we didn't do too well. As explained in the earlier story, the Government of India realized and accepted the poor state of the Indian Army and the immense shortfall in personnel, arms, ammunition and equipment. Orders were issued for the raising of additional units and the 4th Battalion the 5th Gorkha Rifles was ordered for raising at Dehradun. Officers and men would have to be hand-picked from other units of the regiment and no representations would be accepted. On receipt of orders, personnel selected had to move within forty-eight hours. Amongst those who had to move at such short notice were Jumbahadur and me.

On the evening before we left, JCOs, NCOs and men of the battalion came to say goodbye. I had learnt a lot from these wonderful people from the hills of Nepal. They had given me my basic grounding as an officer of the Indian Army and of this illustrious regiment and I felt humbled in their presence. I was filled with a deep sense of loss as I would now not be with them any more.

Jumbahadur's father was there. He had a request for me. He said, 'Captain Sahib, you may be aware that I lost my wife when Jumbahadur was born. We did not have any other children. As long as he was in the battalion, I could watch over him. Now that he is going away, I will not be able to monitor his performance. Since both of you will be in the same battalion, I request you therefore to please take him under your wing.' He then repeated, 'All that I want is that he should be a good soldier and bring honour to the regiment and my family.' I promised his father that I would keep an eye on Jumbahadur and ensure that he would be given every opportunity to become a proficient soldier.

Jumbahadur's father was the Company Havildar Major (CHM) of Alpha Company and I had learnt a lot from him in the few years that we had been together. The next day, it was time to leave. Jumbahadur shook hands with his father. It was an emotional moment for both of them, but like all Gorkhas, they did not give way to their emotions. A firm handshake, a smile and a few words from father to son was all that took place.

Leaving the battalion was a wrench. It had been my home for five years—my most formative years in the army. My mentors had collected to see us off. From each of them I had learnt something about my profession, and the correct attitude, behaviour and conduct as an officer and a gentleman. I had learnt much about the importance of discipline, teamwork, physical fitness, courage, willpower and integrity from these simple men from the hills. I had been to their homes in Nepal on my first leave and been welcomed as part of the regimental family. I had come to know their wives, children and parents. Many of their fathers had served in the regiment and from them I had learnt how the customs and traditions of the regiment had originated and of battles fought by the regiment in far-off lands. From them, I had learnt their language and their dialects, their songs and dances, amid much laughter and good humour. I had also learnt at first-hand, the hard conditions of life in the hills of Nepal.

It was Jumbahadur who had accompanied me on my first visit to Nepal. He too was on his first leave and his was the first home I visited. Jumbahadur's father was at home. As my Company Havildar Major, he had planned it that way. After a couple of days, Jumbahadur escorted me to the next home. Every few days, I was taken to another home by one of the family members and it went on like that, till it was time to return to the battalion.

Now it was time for Jumbahadur and me to make our new home with the battalion that was being re-raised. The 4th Battalion had been raised during World War II and had earned a great name for itself during the Burma campaign. Due to the cutting down of the strength of the army, it had been disbanded. It had been re-raised in the aftermath of the Sino-Indian war and it was now up to us to make this re-raised battalion of the regiment as good as what it was during the Second World War.

Raising the battalion was a learning experience. All the officers and men worked very hard to ensure that the battalion would be as good as any other battalion of the regiment. We were inspected within six months of raising and found fit to serve in an operational area, and were sent to man the border in Jammu and Kashmir.

The battalion manned the border during the years 1963, 1964 and 1965. The Pakistan Army kept us busy and it was practical 'hands-on' training for us. The Pakistani picquets kept firing at us initially, probably to test our battle-worthiness, and in the process, wasted a lot of ammunition. During the early part of 1965, firing from the other side increased dramatically. But we didn't know why.

What intelligence failed to tell us was that Pakistan was hatching plans for a new war to take Jammu and Kashmir by force.

During July 1965, the battalion was brought down from the picquets for training. We were about to commence training when, in the first week of August, Pakistan launched a force of 12,000 guerrillas through the division that was opposite us. The force was led by Pakistan Army officers, JCOs and NCOs.

Our battalion was one of the first units that these guerrillas encountered. We had established a tented camp and posted small security picquets, and a guerrilla column bumped into one of them. Our men opened fire and the guerrillas hastily withdrew, leaving their dead and wounded behind. We were also able to capture a few of them who were sent to the division headquarters for interrogation. The guerrillas revealed that ten columns, each of a thousand guerrillas, had been launched by Pakistan across the CFL under an operation titled 'Operation Gibraltar'.

Since our battalion was the only infantry battalion not holding ground, we therefore, willy-nilly, became the divisional reserve, and we were broken up into company groups to tackle different situations. By this time, Jumbahadur was designated as my batman and runner. In one of the skirmishes with these infiltrators, Jumbahadur got wounded and had to be sent to hospital.

Subsequently, part of my company which was escorting a major convoy between Pathankot and Poonch, and which was being commanded by me, was ambushed by a large group of infiltrators. Some of my men were killed and some wounded. The wounded met Jumbahadur at the hospital and brought him up to date with what was going on.

A group of infiltrators, probably the one which had ambushed the convoy, exfiltrated from the area but uncharacteristically took up a defence position on top of a hill called Gajna.

The battalion was now tasked to capture and destroy this defensive position.

All this was conveyed to Jumbahadur at the military hospital. Jumbahadur began to feel concerned about my safety and well-being. What I did not know at that time was that Jumbahadur had been tasked by his father to protect me and ensure my security at all cost.

Jumbahadur requested the hospital authorities to discharge him and send him back to the battalion.

The hospital authorities refused because his wound had not yet healed fully.

Jumbahadur's concern for me probably overrode the orders of the hospital authorities. He had to decide between obeying the hospital authorities or obeying his father who, in his young mind, was also an army 'authority' as he was a Company Havildar Major, although now in a different battalion.

Jumbahadur decided to obey his father and without permission, left the military hospital. His friends from the battalion, who were also being treated for their wounds, covered up for him and the hospital authorities did not discover for some days that Jumbahadur had gone away. The battalion was, in the meantime, preparing for the capture and destruction of Gajna where the infiltrators had taken a defensive position.

In the early hours of the morning, on the day of the attack, I was busy tying up the last-minute arrangements for the attack, when the Company Havildar Major reported that Jumbahadur was back and that he wanted to take his place as my batman and runner. The Company was short of manpower because of the men who had been killed and wounded in earlier operations and the leave parties which had not yet returned. The strength was just fifty-eight. I clearly remember this figure because it was also the year of my commission. And so Jumbahadur taking his place as my runner meant that one of the sections would be brought up to strength. Also, Jumbahadur knew his job well. I asked whether Jumbahadur was all right and the CHM said, 'Yes'. So, I said, 'OK' and Jumbahadur came up and took over his job as my batman and runner. I had presumed that Jumbahadur had been discharged from the military hospital.

At that moment, while I was talking with Jumbahadur, I was told that the CO wanted all the company commanders for final orders. I told Jumbahadur to take charge of my weapon and binoculars, and I went off to take final orders from the CO for the attack on Gajna.

The CO gave out his final orders and asked if there were any questions. I submitted that there was the possibility of interference from a parallel ridge and that it needed to be secured. The CO directed the artillery battery commander to register it as one of his targets. I gave the battery commander the coordinates of the area and the battalion commenced its advance towards Gajna top. Jumbahadur was carrying my map case and binoculars in addition to his own weapon and equipment.

Due to the heavy casualties suffered by my Company during the ambush, my company was placed in reserve. That meant Alpha Company would not be used to launch the attack but would be used only if necessary, and if required. My Company was therefore at the tail-end of the column and I was part of the CO's 'O' Group, just behind the leading rifle company.

The leading company was advancing up the steep, barren and narrow ridge leading up to Gajna when, just as I had predicted, heavy machine gun fire erupted from the parallel ridge, sweeping the area along which we were advancing.

The leading company halted and took cover behind the rocks available. I wondered what I would do if I was in the place of the CO, when I was surprised to hear him say in Nepali, '*Cardo kasto hola?*' which translated from Nepali meant 'Cardozo, how about it?', i.e., the CO was asking me to take over the assault on Gajna. I took that as an order and told Jumbahadur to tell the CHM to bring the company up. As soon as they arrived, we started to scramble up the hillside.

There was no cover available and the bullets were coming uncomfortably close. Staying where we were, would only be inviting casualties, so we kept moving up the hillside. Jumbahadur was on my left and Lance Naik Jitbahadur, my wireless operator, was on my right. The enemy MMG fire was coming from the ridge to my right and was striking the ground around us. I passed a message on the wireless set to ask for artillery fire on the ridge from where the enemy fire was coming but apparently, we were out of communication with the guns. An MMG burst struck Jitbahadur's wireless set and he told me in a very matter of fact way that his wireless set had got damaged and we were out of communication with the battalion. There was no option except to quickly get away from this area to broken ground ahead, where some cover was available. I got up and ordered my company to follow me. Jumbahadur was at my side. As we were moving up the narrow ridge, the volleys of MMG bullets were coming closer and closer. One bullet passed very close to my face and the zing of its passage close to my ear told me that I had had a really close call. Our artillery did not seem to be able to get its act together and the enemy machine guns were having a field day. I was moving quickly up the slope and the company was following me, when I heard a cry at my side and saw Jumbahadur stumble and fall. He had been hit and was bleeding badly.

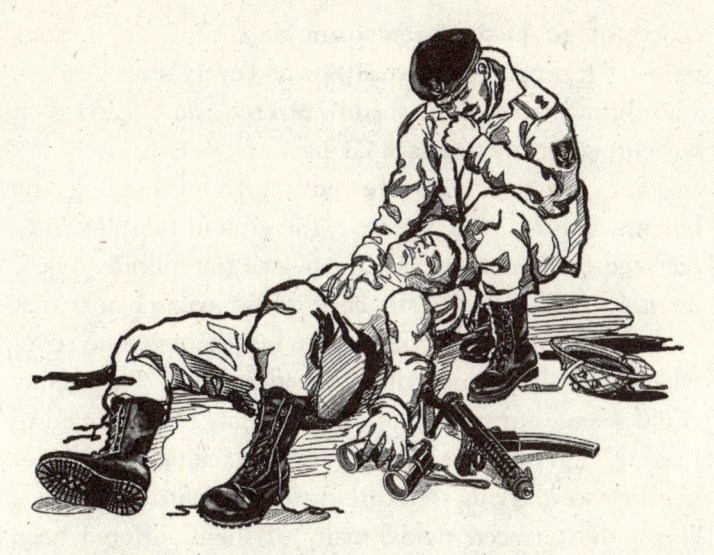

Death of Rifleman Jumbahadur, Battle of Gajna

I was in a dilemma. On the one hand I wanted to attend to Jumbahadur who was badly wounded, but my duty lay not only in the capture of the objective but also to get my company out of harm's way. The present position was too dangerous and any further delay would result in more casualties to the men of my company. Jumbahadur was bleeding from the mouth, which probably meant that he had taken bullets in his chest. I therefore reluctantly asked my Company Havildar Major to see that Jumbahadur was moved away from the zone of fire to a place where cover was available and carried on with my advance for the capture of the hill feature. Much as I wanted to stay with Jumbahadur, I could not. I remembered the words of my platoon commander at the Indian Military Academy who had repeatedly dinned it into the heads of the gentlemen cadets of his platoon that 'your duty comes first, your personal feelings come last, always and every time.' And so, I left Jumbahadur in the shadow of a rock, and I carried on with my company to attack Gajna.

The guerrillas had the advantage of holding the heights. Short of the objective, the ground morphed into terraced fields that had been cut into the hillside. These terraced fields were partly covered by maize plants that offered the enemy adequate cover, but there was no cover whatsoever in the area that we had reached. The enemy could see us, but we could not see them. They seemed to have the latest weapons and lots of machine guns. Since my boys were trying to locate the enemy with their heads above the terraced fields, many of them suffered head injuries. The enemy was able to pick us out with rifle and light machine gun fire. I asked Naib Subedar Prem Singh, the newly promoted JCO, who was next to me, where the fire was coming from. He was indicating the direction, when there was a sudden silence. I looked at him and to my disbelief, saw that he was dead. He had received a bullet in his head.

The enemy was lobbing grenades at us, and they were bouncing down the slopes. Naib Subedar Narbahadur Gurung seemed to be unfazed and was throwing back the enemy grenades. He was an amazing person who seemed to have a charmed life!

Suddenly, there was a major movement among the maize plants and the enemy seemed to be massing for an attack by rushing down the slope. But our boys stood firm and shot their attack to pieces with cries of '*Ayo Gorkhali*', and the guerrillas went back, dragging away their dead and wounded.

I took stock of the situation. We had suffered many casualties—more wounded than dead, but our strength had dwindled further. With grenades exploding, mortar shrapnel flying around and aimed machine gun fire from the side and the top, it was apparent that desperate methods were needed. Rallying the men, I charged along with my company up the hillside with our battle cry of '*Ayo Gorkhali*'. The enemy, seeing us advancing with determination despite the heavy fire, wavered, broke ranks and withdrew to their position on top of the hill. Once again, we had beaten back a force superior to us in number, but our charge was more noise than force. I realized that I neither had the strength to capture the objective nor would I be able to withstand another counter-attack. The dead and wounded were lying all around us.

I took stock of the situation and saw that I needed to be reinforced. The battalion was down below with no idea what the situation was, short of the objective. I had no means of communication because my wireless set was damaged and Jumbahadur, my runner, was badly injured. I decided to send Jitbahadur, my wireless operator, to inform the CO that we had suffered heavy casualties after beating back two counter-attacks and we needed to be reinforced quickly.

Luckily, the message reached in time and Maj. Ashok Mehta came up with Charlie Company, just as the third counter-attack by the enemy was under way, and the enemy was forced to retreat. The arrival of Charlie Company saved the situation.

The rest of the battalion thereafter built up on Alpha and Charlie Companies and consolidated our position on the slope. True to the nature of guerrilla warfare, the guerrillas, faced with a superior force, melted away into the darkness. When Charlie Company launched an attack the next morning, the guerrillas had left.

It was only after the Company had reorganized on the objective and had dug in, that I managed to get back to Jumbahadur but it was too late. Jumbahadur had passed away. He had bled considerably but there was a peaceful look on his face. He was still clutching my binoculars, which was covered with his blood. I felt devastated. Jumbahadur had put his life on the line to watch over me and had made the ultimate sacrifice in deference to his father's orders. I felt sad, very sad, but there were many other issues that had to be dealt with. The dead and wounded had to be evacuated and the Company had to be reorganized for fresh tasks ahead. Being busy helped take away some of the sadness for the time being.

In the meantime, the Military Hospital had sent out a report that Jumbahadur was absent from the hospital without leave (AWOL). The report had gone all the way up the chain of command and all sorts of explanations were asked for. A Court of Inquiry was held after the war and the Military Hospital took a dim view of Jumbahadur's absence from the hospital. They found no merit in the fact that Jumbahadur though wounded, had voluntarily gone back into battle. They wanted to punish him, but they couldn't since he was dead. They, however, apparently felt that since Jumbahadur had died and no action could be taken against him, his Company Commander be conveyed the 'Displeasure' of the competent authority for irresponsible behaviour in allowing Jumbahadur, who was already wounded, to take part in battle. This entire episode made me feel disillusioned. It was as if Jumbahadur and I had done something dishonorable.

Fortunately, the General Officer Commanding the Division took a more balanced view. He exonerated both Jumbahadur and me and commended both of us for taking responsibility in adverse circumstances.

The sanction for Jumbahadur's family pension was more problematic. It took many years to sort out. When a soldier dies in battle, his wife or parents are entitled to a family pension. In Jumbahadur's case, his mother had died in childbirth and his father, who was his only surviving relation, was a serving soldier. Much correspondence flowed between the battalion and higher headquarters up and down the chain of command, the Records Office, the Regimental Centre and the various offices of the Pension Paying Department. The main beneficiary should have been Sarabjit, Jumbahadur's father. 'Babudom', however, felt that since Sarabjit was a paid serving soldier, he could not draw his own pay and also benefit from the family pension of his dead son.

The family pension due to Jumbahadur's father on account of the death in battle of his only son never came through, thanks to an unhelpful and negative bureaucratic mindset. When the sanction finally came through many years later, Sarabjit had passed away and there were now no legal heirs left. Babudom had triumphed, as always, and was happy to close the case.

Postscript

This is a small attempt by a Company Commander to put on record the bravery, loyalty and commitment of a simple Gorkha soldier, who put courage beyond fear and duty above death.

10

Twists of Fate

'War is a place where young people who do not know each other and don't hate each other kill each other, by the decisions of old people who know each other and hate each other, but don't kill each other and shake hands at the end of the war. This is a sad reality and a hard truth which most people are not aware of.'

—Anonymous

This story is about two families—one from India and one from Pakistan—brought together in Australia on a Defence Staff College course. The story starts with a throwback on what happened in the Indo–Pak war of 1965, continues through the intervening years and concludes when their countries go to war in 1971. So essentially it is also a story of two wars.

The ominous signs of decline of relations between the two countries during the Defence Staff College course highlights how this affected the two families—the struggle between love for one's country and the relationship that had developed between the families, and finally, what happens during the war and its aftermath.

Battle at Dera Baba Nanak bridge

6 September 1965, Dera Baba Nanak

It was around 0400 hours on the morning of 6 September 1965. The darkness of night had yet to give way to the greyness of dawn. Brig. Pritam Singh, Commander 29 Indian Infantry Brigade, was busy tying up the details of the conduct of the assault on the bridge at Dera Baba Nanak (DBN). His brigade had been tasked to secure the Pakistani defensive positions on this side of the bridge and if possible, to capture the bridge intact. He was trying to communicate with two of his battalions, 2 Raj Rif and 1/5 GR (FF), but there appeared to be a problem. Notwithstanding his inability to communicate with his units, the battalions knew what they had to do, and went about their tasks in accordance with well-known battle drills.

The 150-metre railroad bridge over the Ravi River was part of a Pakistani enclave which extended 1.6 km into Indian territory and was under the control of Pakistan.[1] It was protected by troops of 3 Punjab of Pakistan's 115 Infantry Brigade and tanks of 30 Cavalry.

DBN marked the northern boundary of India's XI Corps' area of responsibility. The railroad bridge that spanned the Ravi River was important because it linked areas of strategic importance to both India and Pakistan. A small Pakistani enclave existed on the Indian side of the Ravi and a larger Indian enclave extended into Pakistan.

With the opening of the second front in Punjab, XI Corps was tasked to advance and hold the line of the Ichhogil Canal from east to west and to secure all bridges across that canal. This would give the Indian forces the benefit of an obstacle ahead of them and to use the Ichhogil Canal to their own advantage. Capture of the bridges across the Ichhogil Canal and areas forward of it would also give XI Corps the ability to cross the canal at will and threaten Lahore.

Brig. Muzaffaruddin Commander Pakistani 115 Infantry Brigade, was asleep. He was woken up and informed that the Indians were possibly in the process of attacking the defensive positions held by 3 Punjab, which was one of his battalions responsible for holding the bridge. He immediately ordered the firing of defensive fire tasks, but the Indian troops had achieved initial surprise by launching silent attacks. There was confused fighting on the Indian side of the bridge but after half an hour, it was clear that the Indians had the upper hand. 2 Raj Rif and 1/5 GR (FF) had captured their objectives and had moved forward on to the bridge.

The brigadier now ordered a counter-attack with infantry and armour to capture the positions lost to the Indians. The counter-attack was supported by heavy shelling by Pakistani artillery and mortars. The bridge was covered with the haze of smoke and dust generated by the artillery and mortar fire, and the Indian troops could hear the enemy tanks come rumbling across the bridge. They peered through the haze at the oncoming tanks. and prepared to attack them with their handheld rocket launchers.

Perhaps the crews of the Pakistani tanks found it difficult to locate the Indian positions from the inside of their tanks and a young officer came out of his cupola to get a better view of what was going on. He was promptly shot and killed by Capt. Arvind Kumar of the Rajputana Rifles. The remaining two tanks of the troop[2] of Pakistani tanks ground to a halt on the bridge.

2/Lieutenant Harwant Singh of 1/5 GR (FF) saw this as an opportunity. He clambered to the top of one of the enemy tanks that had stopped and wrenching open the turret cover threw a grenade inside, killing its entire crew. He was, however, now exposed, and before he could jump down from the tank, he was riddled with bullets from the machine gun of the third tank. His body crumpled and fell down beside the tank he had just attacked.

A ding-dong battle with Indian infantry versus Pakistani armour and infantry followed, but by 1330 hours, a troop of Indian tanks from 9 Horse arrived and stopped further Pakistani progress. By this time, both the remaining Pakistani tanks had been destroyed by Indian rocket launchers. An Indian counter-attack was launched at 0040 hours on 7 September. Brig. Muzaffaruddin panicked and ordered the blowing up of the bridge.

With the blowing up of the bridge at DBN, the Indians were denied the advantage of using the bridge over the Ravi River. However, with the destruction of the bridge, the right flank of XI Corps was now comparatively safe and 29 Indian Infantry Brigade was ordered to Khem Karan, where a fresh threat was developing.

Capt. Arvind Kumar felt a twinge of sadness for having killed the young Pakistani officer, who by his looks, seemed to be his own age. He, however, remembered the words of his platoon commander at the Indian Military Academy who had said, 'You have joined a band of brothers who live by chance, love by choice and kill by profession. The only good enemy is a dead enemy. Therefore, you need to kill him before he kills you. And you must kill without fear, without pity and without remorse!' That platoon commander, Capt. Desmond Hayde, would go on to win an MVC at Dograi, the capture of which was under way not too far from DBN.

Arvind wondered whether that platoon commander, now probably a lieutenant colonel in command of a battalion, killed without fear, pity and remorse? Saying something was different from carrying it out in person! And although he had killed without a second thought, he felt on reflection that he did feel a little bad. But he put his feelings aside because he accepted that he had killed in the course of duty and perhaps he would kill many more before this war was over. Therefore, perhaps the best he could do for the people he had killed was to see that the bodies of the war dead were given their last rites in accordance with their faiths and to keep a record of what was done.

There was no time to perform these rituals at DBN by Arvind and his Company because they had to move post-haste to Khem Karan. So, Arvind passed a message to Vinodh, the battalion quartermaster, who though senior, was a captain like him, to do what was necessary in accordance with the rituals of the war dead, and confirm that this had been done. Eventually, that confirmation was received only after the war was over and by that time, his battalion had fought two more battles and he had killed many more of the enemy. His own batman had been killed by his side along with many more from his Company and it became clear to him that in war, it was 'survival of the fittest'. You had to kill or be killed!

Sunday, 12 July 1970, Rawalpindi

Five years later, Maj. Ahmed Khan, an officer of the 32nd Khyber Rifles was browsing through the Sunday edition of *Dawn* looking for the Staff College results that were to be published that day. He found them at the bottom right-hand corner of page 5. He quickly scanned through the column and found his name among the first three of the successful candidates. He couldn't believe his eyes and he called out excitedly to his wife, 'Miriam, the staff college results are out and my name is at number three! This means that I will go abroad to do the staff course!'

Miriam, who was making breakfast, came running to the veranda with a ladle in her hand to find out why her husband was so excited. Ahmed could not restrain his joy and kept dancing around. Miriam said, 'Hush, you'll wake up the children.' But the children were already awake and came out in their nightclothes, rubbing the sleep out of their eyes to see what the excitement was all about. They were astonished to see their father prancing about on the veranda.

Miriam sent the children in to brush their teeth and wash their faces. She told Ahmed to calm down and not get so excited, and that he should wait for orders to tell him whether he would go abroad or do the course at Quetta. 'Better to wait and not jump to conclusions, otherwise you might be disappointed,' she said.

Friday, 7 August 1970, 0800 hours, Mathura

Nearly a month later, a similar development was taking place at Mathura Cantonment in India. Arvind Kumar, who was now a major, was doing a staff job at a formation headquarters and had gone early to his office on his scooter. He had just entered his office when his phone started ringing. He picked up the receiver and was surprised to learn that it was a telephone call from Delhi, from a brigadier who had recently been posted out of the formation headquarters. 'Hello, Arvind,' he said. 'Congratulations. Have you seen today's papers?'

'No, Sir,' said Arvind.

'Well, I have the *Times of India* in front of me, and the staff college results are out at page 4. Your name is at the top of the list of competitive vacancies and that means you should be going abroad.'

'Thank you, Sir,' stammered Arvind. He could not believe that he had topped the list! He knew that he had done well but did not expect that he would have done so well.

The brigadier was still on the line. 'Well done, Arvind. This merits a party the next time we meet. You had better give Nalini the good news.'

'Yes, Sir. Thank you, Sir,' said Arvind as the brigadier terminated the call.

Arvind rang up the house and Nalini answered. 'Yes Arvind, what is it?'

Arvind tried to keep his excitement out of his voice. He said, 'Nalini, have the newspapers come?'

'Yes,' she said.

'I have been told the Staff College results are out. Can you look for it? It should be on page 4.'

After a while, Nalini answered. 'Yes. It is here.'

'What does it say?'

Nalini said, 'The heading says "DSSC Examination Results" and goes on to say, "Competitive Vacancies" and then your name is number one in the competitive list.'

'OK. Thanks! I'm just coming home. Have the children gone to school?'

'Yes,' she replied.

Arvind got on to his scooter and rushed home to explain to Nalini what those words in the newspaper meant.

January 1971, Singapore Airport

By the early sixties, Singapore had become the centre of the world for intercontinental air travel between the east and the west. All long-distance flights to Australia, New Zealand, Japan, Taiwan, Korea and the Philippines stopped for a break at Singapore. Arvind, Nalini and their children, Naomi and Arjun, were travelling to Australia. Arvind had been selected to do the Staff College course at Queenscliff, Australia, because he was high on the Indian merit list for the Defence Services Staff College entrance exam. Since the course was for a year, officers' families were allowed to accompany the officer. Travel abroad was an education in itself and so Naomi, who was ten years old and Arjun, who was two years younger, were pulled out of their schools in India to do a year's schooling in Australia. Naomi wanted to be a doctor like her mother, and Arjun wanted to follow his father into the Army and into the Rajputana Rifles. To them, the regiment was 'family'.

The Australian Command and Staff College, also known as Queenscliff Staff College, was located at Fort Queenscliff, Victoria, Australia. The college trains officers from Australia and various other countries. Arvind and his family were waiting for their connecting flight to take them to Melbourne, which was the airport closest to the college.

While they were waiting in the lounge, the airport intercom announced that a Pakistani International Airways (PIA) flight had just landed and could those waiting for a connecting flight please report to the help desk?

A little later, a family of four walked into the lounge. Soldiers the world over are recognizable by the way they look, walk and talk, and it was clear that this was an army officer and his family. By the way they dressed and looked, it was also clear that this was a family from Pakistan. The children—a girl and a boy—were about the same ages as Arvind and Nalini's children and could have passed off as children from India. Arvind wondered if this was the Pakistani officer who would be doing the course with him at Queenscliff. Arvind and the Pakistani officer sized each other up. Neither made the first move to meet and greet each other. After all, they were *'dushman'* and had fought a vicious war just five years earlier in the Indo–Pak war of 1965.

It remained for the women to make the first move, and it was the Pakistani woman who came across and introduced herself, saying, 'Good afternoon. I am Miriam and my husband is going to Australia for an army course. You look like army folk. Are you heading for the same course?' Arvind stood up and answered, 'Good afternoon, Ma'am. I am Major Arvind Kumar from the Indian Army. This is my wife Nalini and those are our children, Naomi and Arjun. Yes, we are going for the staff course at Queenscliff.'

By this time, the children were making friends with each other and started happily playing together. The man walked up and introduced himself as Major Ahmed from the Khyber Rifles, Pakistan Army.

During the conversation that followed, it transpired that both the women were doctors and both the men were from rifle regiments.

All four had the same thought. How strange that both the women were doctors and both the men were from rifle regiments! However, after a while, they learnt that although Nalini was a doctor of medicine, Miriam was a doctor of literature and that the names of the Pakistani children were Fatima and Adil.

Their conversation was interrupted by an announcement that said, '*Transients travelling to Melbourne by Air India need to move to Gate No. C-22.*' The men shook hands and the families parted with a resolve to catch up at Queenscliff.

Meeting of two Service families—Indian and Pakistani

1971, Queenscliff

Queenscliff was a two-hour drive from Melbourne airport. In layout and design, it was similar to other staff colleges of Commonwealth countries the world over. It had an auditorium, classrooms called syndicate rooms, sand-model rooms, an officers' mess, living quarters for both bachelors and married officers, a gym, a swimming pool and an officers' club. Outdoor exercises were held in and around the hills and plains in the vicinity of the college.

Officers' family quarters consisted of a line of row houses. Arvind and Ahmed were located at the opposite ends of the colony. Perhaps the Aussies thought that the Indians and Pakistanis needed to be kept apart as far as possible! The children's school was walking distance from the family quarters. The college was happy to have Miriam, a qualified teacher, to take Class VI and to have Nalini take on the responsibility of the medical officer of the college. Although the living quarters of Arvind and Ahmed were far apart, the children were in and out of each other's houses most of the time.

April 1971, Queenscliff

Sometime around April 1971, disturbing reports began to be reported in the Australian newspapers, which stated that East Pakistan was in ferment and the Pakistani military had cracked down on the civilian people of East Pakistan who were advocating for freedom from Pakistani misrule. The reports stated that a large number of people from

East Pakistan had been massacred and there was a mass exodus of refugees crossing over into India. Some of the reports called the killings a 'genocide.' It was evident that the Pakistan Army was putting down the revolt with an iron hand, but the news reports stated that the repressive measures included rape and murder. It was also reported that two more infantry divisions were flown into East Pakistan. These infantry formations had to fly into East Pakistan via Sri Lanka as India refused to give permission for them to fly over Indian territory. By the end of April, over ten million refugees had taken sanctuary in India. This was causing political, economic and social problems for India.

June 1971, Queenscliff

The mid-term break took place in the middle of June 1971 and an excursion was organized to a resort not far from Queenscliff. Being in the southern hemisphere, Australian winters take place when the rest of the world is sweltering from the summer heat. Arvind and Ahmed and their families were sitting around a fire and Miriam spoke about the vicissitudes of war. She said, 'I lost my brother in the 1965 war. It happened at a place called Dera Baba Nanak.'

Arvind was taken aback. He held his breath and wondered what she would say next.

Miriam continued, 'He was a captain in the armoured corps and was serving with 30 Cavalry. He was defending the bridge at DBN. All that we know is that he was killed and that his body was never recovered. We do not know whether his last rites were carried out, which is a cause of great concern to my family.'

Arvind was shaken by this revelation by Miriam. He realized that it was probably her brother that he had killed five years ago at DBN! What sense would it make to tell her that he was only doing his duty and it was unfortunate that her brother had to die at his hands? What could he say?

Arvind listened quietly without revealing the part he had played in this tragic drama. He finally spoke. He said that the Indian Army was very particular about maintaining ethics in war and that one of the issues it emphasized was the proper disposal of the enemy war dead in accordance with the religious rites of the personnel concerned. He said that it was strange, but his own unit was involved in the fighting at DBN and he would find out if they had any knowledge of whether the last rites were given to the Pakistani war dead at DBN.

Arvind knew that this had been done, but a revelation at this stage would show that he knew more than he was revealing about what happened on that day so many years ago. He wrote to Vinodh, the Unit second-in-command who was the quartermaster at that time, and who had carried out the burial service of the Pakistani war dead at DBN during the 1965 war. Arvind explained his predicament and asked him to write back regarding the last rites given to the Pakistani dead at DBN.

Vinodh who was now the second-in-command of the Unit wrote back to say:

Dear Arvind,

Hope you are studying hard and doing well in the Staff College course at Queenscliff.

Wonder whether you are aware of what is happening in East Pakistan? Hordes of refugees—more than ten million, have crossed over from East Pakistan into our states of Tripura, West Bengal and Odisha due to mass killings by the Pakistan Army of the citizens of East Pakistan who were agitating for self-rule. The situation is going from bad to worse and we do not know how all this is going to end!

Yes, we did carry out the necessary rituals of the Pakistani soldiers who were killed at DBN. One of them was an officer. His name is Captain Aslam Beg. We have the identity discs[3] of those who were killed and would be happy to send them to the people concerned. We had approached GHQ Pakistan but received no reply. It would be good if we could close the chapter on this episode.

On receiving the letter, Arvind met Ahmed and Miriam and shared it with them. The conversation went something like this:

'Miriam, what was your brother's name? Was it Aslam Beg?'

Miriam's eyes opened wide with surprise. She replied, 'Yes. How do you know?'

Arvind explained that he had received a response to his letter and revealed to Miriam and Ahmed that the last rites had indeed been carried out in accordance with the Muslim rites for burial and that they were performed by an Indian Army maulvi from a neighbouring unit.

Miriam began to cry and was comforted by Ahmed. When she had recovered sufficiently, she thanked Arvind and asked whether she could get the identity discs of her brother so that she could give them to her parents and reassure them that Aslam's last rites had indeed been performed by an Indian Muslim maulvi. Hopefully, it would bring closure to this sad episode.

2 August 1971, Queenscliff

On 2 August 1971, Miriam received a telegram from Pakistan stating that her father was critically ill and that he desired to see his daughter before he passed away. Miriam was distraught. She realized how much this meant to her father and to her, but her duty lay with her husband and her children here in Australia.

Knowing the struggle that was going on within her, Nalini spoke to Miriam and said, 'Miriam, if you have to go, please go. You don't have to worry about the children. Send them to me. I will look after them till you return. Ahmed can have his meals with us if he wishes.' And this is exactly how it happened.

Fatima and Adil moved in with Nalini and Arvind. The children were very excited and happy at the new experience of living in someone else's home. It was like an extended sleepover! Ahmed came for dinner every evening to meet up with his children and had his breakfast and lunch in the officers' mess. He could not move in with Arvind and Nalini as the rules did not permit it. As it was, permission had to be obtained from the college authorities for Fatima and Adil to move in with the Kumars till Miriam returned.

By the time Miriam came back to Queenscliff, the children had become very close. Miriam and Nalini too, because Nalini had been a mother to her children while she was away.

Miriam came to Nalini's home to collect her children and was surprised to find that the children were very happy with the present arrangement. They asked why couldn't Miriam and Ahmed also move in with Nalini and Arvind?

Nalini had taken pains to ensure that Fatima and Adil did not miss their mother. She saw that they finished their homework and had their baths on time. She personally washed their clothes and pressed them and had them ready for school every day. She also found out about their prayers and ensured that they said them in the morning and in the evening. Cast, creed, nationality and all other differences seemed to melt away in the warm embrace of love and concern for each other. Children are children the world over and in God's eyes, there is no difference—at least there wasn't to Nalini, Arvind, Ahmed, Miriam and the children.

20 October 1971, Queenscliff

Meanwhile, the situation on the border between India and East Pakistan had gone from bad to worse. The freedom fighters of East Pakistan known as the Mukti Bahini were using guerrilla tactics to trouble the Pakistan Army from their bases in India, and Yahya Khan, the President and Army Chief of Pakistan, was threatening to go to war with India for sheltering and training the Mukti Bahini. It appeared that, given the situation at that time, war was inevitable.

Information was also received from India and Pakistan that personnel on leave were being recalled and training courses were being terminated ahead of time. Ahmed was told that his posting on the staff would be kept on hold and that he should rejoin his unit latest by 25 November. The date of joining given to Ahmed helped Arvind conclude that the war would not start before 25 November and Arvind shared this information with his battalion. He too was told to join his battalion latest by the third week of November after taking his family home.

The course at Queenscliff was scheduled to terminate in the first week of December 1971, but Arvind and Ahmed had to leave for India and Pakistan, respectively, latest by 15 November, so that they could join their respective units on time, i.e., before the commencement of a war that appeared inevitable. Their respective country authorities had asked for permission from the college to release Arvind and Ahmed by that date. The college asked whether they could use the same van to take them to the airport. Both Arvind and Ahmed agreed as it would give the families more time to be together.

15 November 1971, Queenscliff

15 November was the date fixed for both Arvind and Ahmed to return to their respective countries. Both Arvind and Ahmed were given a farewell dinner the previous night by their course mates. It was a strange situation. The students at the course knew that India and Pakistan were not on the best of terms and were likely to go to war, and here a different story seemed to be evolving!

The mood on the journey to the airport was sombre and quiet. Uppermost in their respective minds was the fact that it appeared that war was inevitable, considering the statements of Gen. Yahya Khan who had said, 'In ten days I will be off fighting a war!' and 'I shall teach India a lesson that she will never forget.' All this was being reported in the newspapers.

Arvind and Ahmed were both cogitating on the futility of war. Pakistan had twice tried to wrest J & K from India in 1947–48 and in 1965 and had failed. This time, it was clear that Pakistan was once more 'upping the ante' by conducting a holocaust in East Pakistan and it was clear to all that it would not work and that many would die before Pakistan came to its senses. Neither Arvind nor Ahmed commented on what was happening in East Pakistan. What could they share? They were on opposite sides! Their countries would soon be going to war and where did that place them in relation to each other? The wives and the children also understood that there was the possibility of a war and that Arvind and Ahmed would be fighting in that war. God forbid they would be fighting each other!

Both families parted company at the airport as both had to embark on different airlines and from different gates. The parting was sad. They had become very close to one another from the time they first met at Singapore Airport and now they would part, perhaps never to see each other again. It had been a journey of nine months since they first met and much had happened along the way. During this period, the wives and children in particular had grown very attached and now it was all over! Or was it? One never knew whether this war would take place and what would be the consequences for both the families and the nations they belonged to!

23 November 1971, Rawalpindi

On 22 November 1971, Gen. Yahya Khan, President of Pakistan and Pakistan's Army Chief, called for an operational conference the next day, i.e., 23 November. Those who were called were the Strike Corps commanders, the Pakistani Air Chief and the principal staff officers who included the Chief of General Staff, Director of Military Operations, the Quartermaster General, Director Armoured Corps, Director Infantry and others. Strangely, the Naval Chief was missing! The composition for the conference indicated that this was an operational meeting that would decide the future course of the war. It was also probable that the fatal date Pakistan planned to go to war against India would also be decided.

23 November 1971, New Delhi

Strangely, at Delhi, a similar meeting had been ordered by the Chiefs of Staff Committee at 11 a.m. on 23 November. The commanders-in-chief of the three services were called upon to brief their respective service chiefs in the presence of the Raksha Mantri and the Defence Secretary. In this way, all who were present got to know the plans of the three services and all loose ends could be tied up. The return of the refugees was the core issue. From the discussions, it had become clear that the refugees could return only if

East Pakistan was liberated and that too was contingent on the destruction of the Pakistani war machine. War plans had been made and approved for the eastern and western fronts. All that was now left was to know when the war would commence!

25 November 1971

By the fourth week of November, both Arvind and Ahmed had joined their units. Ahmed's unit was somewhere in POK (Pakistan Occupied Kashmir) and Arvind's unit was on the border in the Poonch Sector. Ahmed was asked to report to his battalion's rear area at Kotli and he would get further instructions from there. Kotli is close to Poonch and Ahmed figured out that his unit would be located somewhere in the Poonch Sector.

A Jeep awaited Arvind at Jammu Railway Station and he was driven to his battalion rear area.

Both officers were extremely glad to be reunited with their battalions and all misgivings on the cause, conduct and consequences of the war were banished from their minds as they renewed the bonds of friendship with their officers and men and prepared for war. Now that they were in their own unit areas, from all information that was available, it was quite clear that India and Pakistan were going to be at war in a short while with 'no holds barred'. Only the date of the commencement of the war was not known, but it was clear that the day was very close.

November was cold and night falls early in the north. As Ahmed tucked himself into his sleeping bag, he wondered whether Miriam, Fatima and Adil were already asleep and whether they had prayed for him. He also thought about Arvind and wondered where he had moved to. Little did he know that they were in the same sector, and just a few miles separated them from each other!

Meanwhile, Arvind had reached his battalion. He was posted back to his old company. The men were delighted to have him back and he was very happy to be with them again. Some of the riflemen had become NCOs and some of the NCOs had become JCOs—otherwise there was not much change. His journey from Jammu took him through Akhnur, Rajouri, Bhimber Galli, Mendhar and Balnoi. He had served in this area earlier, as a young company officer on a picquet opposite the formidable feature of Dharuchian and he shuddered at the thought of ever having to scale its vertical rockface.

Arvind spent the whole day taking charge of his rifle company and was briefed on all its operational tasks. His company was located on a feature called Gutrian. He was informed that the Brigade Commander, Commander 93 Infantry Brigade, was responsible for the defence of Poonch and that he had four battalions under his command.[4] He had directed each battalion commander to make offensive plans to capture ground across the CFL to be implemented as and when required. Arvind was informed that an additional brigade would be inducted in the event of a war and that was good, considering that earlier on, troops were quite thin on the ground.[5]

By 1 December, Arvind had rehearsed all possible contingencies his company might have to carry out for defensive as well as offensive operations. His post was the highest and most important location in his battalion-defended area and was designated as the ground of tactical importance[6] of his brigade. After a tiring day, he came out of his bunker and looked across the Poonch Valley. It was a moonlit night and the rivers and nullahs reflected the silvery light of the moon. He looked up at the star-spangled sky. It was a beautiful sight and he gave an inward sigh at the possible violence that would soon erupt in this beautiful valley.

Meanwhile, Ahmed was involved with his own company, battalion and brigade tasks. He was informed that his battalion, as part of Pakistani 26 Infantry Brigade, was part of an offensive to capture the high ground across the river and that his company was in reserve for the capture of a feature called Gutrian.

Poonch lies in the valley of the Poonch River which takes off from the Pir Panjal range and flows southwards till it joins the Jhelum River. Indian troops were holding defensive positions on the various ridges that dominated the Poonch Valley and Pakistani troops were holding similar defended areas on their side of the valley. From August 1971 onwards, heavy vehicle movements were observed on the Pakistani side. It appeared that a heavy build-up was taking place and that a Pakistani attack on Poonch was likely.

Gen. Yahya Khan had, at the operational conference of 23 November, given the date when Pakistan would go to war with India and that fateful date was 3 December 1971!

Although it was known that Pakistan was gearing up for war, it was not known to India how, when and where she would attack. Indira Gandhi, the Indian Prime Minister, was in Calcutta on 3 December attending a political rally. Defence Minister Jagjivan Ram and Swaran Singh, the Minister for External Affairs, were also away from Delhi when Pakistan attacked Indian airfields at 5.45 p.m.

Ground attacks were also launched in the western sector. Pakistani troops started heavy shelling of the Poonch defences on 3 December 1971 at about 2000 hours and followed up with strong simultaneous attacks on Indian defensive positions. The ferocity and repeated nature of the attacks indicated that Pakistan would be making a determined effort to capture Poonch this time.

Pakistan's 26 Infantry Brigade along with 2 POK and 3 POK Brigade were to capture Poonch by 5 December. 26 Infantry Brigade was tasked to capture features called Gutrian, Shahpur and Thanpir. Arvind was the Company Commander holding one of the Company localities.

At about 2000 hours, Gutrian, Shahpur and Thanpir came under heavy enemy artillery fire. Arvind had firefighting teams ready to put out the fires that would invariably break out because they were at pine-tree level. The pine needles on the ground would catch fire, endangering the bunkers, and would serve as lighted targets for Pakistani forward observation officers to bring down accurate artillery fire on the Indian positions. Arvind waited for the infantry assault to follow the artillery bombardment and ordered his men to hold their fire till the enemy reached their defensive minefield and barbed wire. When they came close, they opened up with their rifles, light and medium machine guns and mortars. The Pakistani attack was beaten back in the minefield itself.

At about 2330 hours, Arvind's Company was once again subjected to heavy artillery fire. Realizing the importance of Gutrian and that its capture was vital for the success of the overall offensive, the enemy put in another attack with a company that attacked from a different direction. This time, the enemy managed to reach the forward defences of Gutrian. Ahmed was the Company Commander and was killed while leading the assault. Confused fighting took place with war cries of both sides intermingling with each other. The battle was ferocious, with bayonets and small arms being used to destroy each other. Ultimately, the attack on all the Indian posts were beaten back, with both sides suffering heavy casualties. Enemy dead bodies littered the Indian defences. Ahmed was there, dead from many bullets. He had led the attack bravely and carried on with the momentum of his charge, bearing the bullets in his young body till he dropped dead. Those who survived withdrew from the location carrying back their dead and wounded. Arvind did not know it was Ahmed who had led the attack and had died in the attempt.

Arvind was reorganizing his Company's defences when the enemy artillery shelled his post Gutrian for the third time. He was outside his bunker and suffered serious injuries from the shelling. Splinters from an artillery shell pierced his lungs and heart and he was bleeding badly. His company was preparing for the next enemy attack, which, however, did not materialize. The battalion regimental medical officer (RMO) was asked to come from the battalion headquarters, which was not too far away, but by the time he arrived, Arvind had passed away.

By the third week of December, the Pakistan Army on the eastern front had suffered a decisive defeat and surrendered on 16 December 1971. After their surrender, India unilaterally stopped operations in the western sector on 17 December 1971 and declared a universal ceasefire in the west. The war came to a close on the intervention of the UN.

Whereas on the eastern front, East Pakistan was liberated and Bangladesh was born, on the western front there was no change and everything reverted to square one. An agreement was concluded between the two countries at Shimla known as the Shimla Agreement and the Line of Control was delineated on 11 December 1972 in Jammu and Kashmir. India returned 13,309 sq. km to Pakistan and received 916 sq. km in return. Over 93,000 Pakistani prisoners were repatriated and the heads of state decided to reopen diplomatic relations between the two countries. Arvind and Ahmed were among those who sacrificed their lives for their respective countries but with the return of the captured territories and the Pakistani prisoners of war, nothing had materially changed on the ground and life went back to what it was earlier.

A flag meeting and memorial service was held on the Line of Control in the Poonch Sector after the war sometime in April 1972, to honour the war dead of both countries and the families of those who had died were invited to attend. Arvind was honoured with the award of the Maha Vir Chakra and Ahmed with the Hilal-i-Jurat.

Unknown to each other, Miriam and Nalini had both chosen to attend the memorial service in order to see the place where their husbands had died. Neither of them knew that the closeness of Arvind and Ahmed in peace had terminated in closeness in death as well. It was better that they did not know, as the knowledge of how they died would be too traumatic for them to understand and accept. Many other families of both sides were present at the memorial service—all grieving for their dead.

A temporary structure was made to honour the war dead from both countries with flags of India and Pakistan on poles and a pandit and maulvi present to offer prayers for the dead. The Brigade Commanders of both sides were there as well as officers and men who had taken part in the war. Buglers of both countries played the 'Last Post'[7] followed by the 'Rouse'[8] with honour guards from both countries doing the honours. It was a solemn moment for all who were present and many of the families broke down in grief at the loss of their loved ones. It was a moment of loss and also a moment of truth, and the truth was that war did not solve any problems. On the contrary, it only created new ones.

Miriam did not know that Nalini was there and Nalini was also oblivious of Miriam's presence.

On conclusion of the service, it was the children who first noticed one another and could not restrain themselves from running across. The mothers followed. Miriam and Nalini clasped each other, sobbing out their shared grief. There was a hush all round and all conversation stopped as this new drama unfolded, which no one could understand. It was inexplicable how two families of countries who were at war with each other could be so close to each other at the same time! Time stopped still and there was no sound except the *shush*[9] of the breeze that wafted through the pine trees while a dog barked somewhere in the valley below.

The two widows in white clung tightly to each other. Those who had assembled watched in awe and silence at the scene. 'Why did this happen to us?' they asked. 'Has our God failed us or have we failed ourselves? Why did we have to go to war? Why was our happiness stolen from us? What have we done to deserve this? What will happen to our children?' There was no answer to their questions and they kept clinging to each other—two women who had come so close to each other in faraway Australia, only to be widowed after they returned home! The children put aside their own grief and tried to comfort their mothers but to no avail. This sudden meeting was too much for Miriam and Nalini, who were finding it hard to understand what had happened.

Finally, the two Brigade Commanders signalled each other, came forward and gently separated the two women. They were unaware of the background to their relationship, but they understood the tragic loss. There was scarcely a dry eye in the crowd. Even the stoic soldiers were affected by the deep sense of loss that had engulfed the assembly.

Miriam and Nalini embraced in a last hug, knowing that this was the last time they would meet. The children too understood the finality of the situation. It was an emotional moment. They wiped the tears from their eyes and said goodbye—a farewell not only to the present but also to the past. The future was unknown but they trusted in God to take care of them and their children.

Postscript

Although all the stories in this book are about the 1965 war, this story, as you would have seen, has a connect with both the 1965 as well as the 1971 wars. Most of the story is true, however, there are some parts which are from my own imagination which help link the families and the two wars together. The names of the characters have been changed to protect their privacy and some of the names of the locations have also been changed. All parts of the story are from conversations with war veterans and from the open domain. The author has not used any information from official sources.

Poonch has figured as an attractive objective in all the wars we have fought with Pakistan. In 1947-48, during the longest war fought between us, Pakistan besieged Poonch for over a year but failed to capture it. In 1965 as well as in 1971, they made determined attempts to capture Poonch but failed. Poonch remains an important strategic objective for Pakistan and will figure in the next conflict as well.

This story brings out the futility of war—particularly in our subcontinent where the two countries fight, where many lives are lost—and then after the war, territories captured are given back, peace agreements are signed, diplomatic relations are re-established and everything goes back to normal.

11

Badmash

'The madness of daring is the wisdom of life.'

—Maxim Gorky

It was the beginning of January 1966. The 1965 war with Pakistan had concluded a few months earlier and an uneasy truce prevailed over the Cease-Fire Line (CFL) of Jammu and Kashmir (J & K). The 'so-called' peace was interrupted every night by the incessant chatter of Pakistani machine guns and the crash of their mortars. The Pakistanis appeared to be jittery over imaginary attacks and they thus continued to keep the tension alive.

On the morning of 4 January, my battalion, the 4th Battalion the 5th Gorkha Rifles, awaited the visit of the newly appointed commander of our brigade.

The previous Brigade Commander had been removed for incompetence and poor leadership during the war. He and our Commanding Officer (CO) had not been able to see eye to eye on many issues. On one occasion, when we were about to launch an attack, the Brigade Commander ordered our CO to come back to the brigade headquarters for a briefing. The CO bluntly reminded him that in such situations, it is the higher formation commander who needs to move forward and not the other way round. A number of similar issues put the previous Brigade Commander and our CO on a collision course and it was the battalion that suffered. The previous Brigade Commander made sure that no recommendations for awards for the battalion were forwarded to higher headquarters, despite the good work that we had done during the war. We felt bad but there was nothing we could do about it.

The new Brigade Commander decided to visit the battalions and make his own assessment. He was now on his first visit to our battalion which was holding a line of picquets in the hill sector of Jammu.

In view of the sacking of the previous commander and in order to impose his personality on the brigade, the new commander made it known to all his commanding officers that his orders would be carried out to the letter and without question and that he would not accept failure of any kind in the execution of his orders. The commanding officers, while appreciating that they could now hope to get clear orders, also felt that the new commander had been influenced by the previous commander. All they could do was wait and hope for the best.

As one of the company commanders of our battalion, I had been detailed to brief the new Brigade Commander. I had got engaged, a few days before the 1965 war. I had requested leave to make arrangements for my wedding, which was scheduled to take place in three months' time. My leave had been sanctioned but was cancelled at the last minute, due to the visit of the new commander. I was not too happy about it, but orders were orders! My picquet had a spectacular view of the enemy territory as far as the eye could see and my briefing would therefore have some significance.

That day, 4 January 1966, dark clouds covered the sky, but rays of sunlight shafted through gaps in the clouds that lit up the patchwork of green and gold fields that lay in what is called Pakistan Occupied Kashmir (POK). The route to our picquets from the base involved a climb of about 2000 ft.

It was a cold morning and the Brigade Commander arrived at the post after a hard climb. He was given a mug of hot tea on arrival and taken to a vantage point from where I could brief him. Somewhere in the middle distance, towards the west, a Pakistani supply point was clearly visible. Vehicles had lined up and when viewed through binoculars, the Brigade Commander could see Pakistani soldiers busy loading their vehicles.

I commenced my briefing. I briefed him about the ground in front of us, the enemy dispositions, the pattern of their activities and our contingency plans. The Commander, instead of paying attention to my briefing, seemed fascinated by the activities at the Pakistani supply point. After I had finished my briefing, he turned to me with a toothy smile. 'Young man', he said, 'If you raid that supply point, I will give you a Maha Vir Chakra.'

I was silent for a moment. I was irritated by the inattentiveness of the Brigade Commander. My leave had been cancelled just for this briefing and the Commander appeared to be more interested in what was going on at the Pakistani supply point. The supply point was about 15 miles as the crow flies. On the ground, it would be much more. It would involve infiltrating through the Pakistani posts and their minefields lower down on the next ridge line, moving approximately 20 miles at night through enemy-held territory and returning after the raid, by which time all the Pakistani posts would have been alerted and would be waiting to destroy us. All things considered, it was a suicidal mission. I wondered whether the Brigade Commander was intentionally giving me an impossible task to test me or whether he had not comprehended the difficulty of the mission. At the back of my mind was the fact that the brigade had dealt with our battalion very unfairly with regard to the matter of awards during the recently concluded war and here was another example of an unfair order. However, the honour of the battalion was at stake.

I answered; 'Sir, my battalion does not work for awards. Give me the task and it will be done.'

The Brigade Commander was taken aback by my reply. He turned around to the CO and addressing him by name, said, 'Madan, you have a very impertinent company commander here. Is this the way your officers talk to their superiors?'

Col. Madan Bhatia, the CO, was a man of honour and never intimidated by rank. He was well-off at home and continued to serve in the Army because he loved its way of life, its customs and traditions, and the need for discipline, courage and competence. He too felt that the Commander was giving me an unreasonable task. He was standing at the back and listening to the briefing and quietly puffing on his pipe. He answered in a matter-of-fact tone with the faint suspicion of a smile, 'Sorry, Sir, but you asked for it.'

This infuriated the Brigade Commander even more. Turning to me, he said. 'Do you see the enemy post in front of you? I want your plans for its capture within a week.'

The enemy post indicated by the Commander was a post that was nicknamed 'Badmash' by our men. It was a post held by a platoon of Pakistani regulars and a contingent of razakars. Razakars were local men from the village behind the post who were armed and trained as irregular soldiers. The post was located on a knoll at the end of a ridge that ran perpendicular to us. The Gorkhas had nicknamed the enemy post 'Badmash' because these irregular soldiers used to come across at night and harass villagers on the Indian side of the CFL.

'Did you hear me?' asked the Brigade Commander.

'Yes, Sir,' I said. 'I will give you my plan within a week.'

The briefing having finished, the CO requested the Brigade Commander to speak to the troops. The Commander addressed those who were available. There was a patrol out at that time and a protection party for the Commander was on 'Stand by', and there were men at their posts watching enemy movements, so there were not too many soldiers available to listen to the Brigade Commander. He was not too happy about this either. He too was from the Gorkhas but from a different regiment. He spoke to the men in Nepali. After he had finished speaking, the CO invited him for lunch. The Brigade

Commander turned down the invitation—probably to indicate that he was not happy and left in a huff. His attitude seemed to indicate that the previous commander was right—these battalion commanders and their officers were too cocky and needed to be sorted out.

The CO felt bad that he had not been able to use this opportunity to build bridges with the Brigade Commander but the honour and integrity of his battalion were more important. He told me to work out my plan and ask for any help that I might need.

My leave was postponed once again!

I was conscious that I had just a week to work out my plan and present it to the Brigade Commander. I could clearly see the enemy post from my forward platoon but the ground around and below the post was invisible. I realized that I might have to go forward to get a better idea of the ground.

I spent the next few days visiting the posts to the left and right to get a better view of the ground around the enemy post, but the pine trees masked the area around Badmash and the visits did not reveal any additional information.

I got down to studying the one-inch map of the area. However, it did not give me the details I desired. All that the contour lines on the map told me was that the post was located on a knoll at the end of the ridge that was perpendicular to the ridge on which my company was located. This, I already knew. What I wanted to know was whether there were suitable approaches to the post from the east, west and from the rear. I felt that a reconnaissance of the ground around Badmash would be inevitable and that I would have to take permission to move forward of my post towards the CFL. I rang up the CO but he had gone to the brigade headquarters and there were no mobiles in those days.

The CFL was a line drawn on the map which indicated the areas in control of India and Pakistan respectively when fighting ceased during the Indo–Pak war of 1947–48. Small boundary pillars marked the CFL on the ground.

I spent the next few days trying to make my plan with whatever information was available. I felt that it was feasible, but it involved an approach about which I needed more information. I knew that if my plan had to be implemented, it was critical that I got better information about the approach that I would finally take.

Three days later, early on the morning of 7 January, before darkness turned to light, I was at the forward platoon locality at 'Stand to'. Only one day was left before I had to submit my plan to the Brigade Commander.

'Stand to' is a drill organized at all picquets before dawn and dusk to help troops familiarize themselves with the ground in front of them. Sentries at night, alone at their posts, tend to sometimes imagine that a bush moving in the breeze could be an enemy soldier. 'Stand to' drills at dusk help the soldier to identify during daylight every rock and bush in front of him as to what it actually is, so that at night he doesn't get confused. 'Stand to' drills at dawn help search the ground in front of the post to confirm that the enemy has not come close to the post under the cover of darkness to launch a surprise attack.

That morning, as the darkness of night faded into the greyness of dawn, the sentry at the forward post indicated that some movement was taking place close to the CFL. The curtain of the early morning mist was just lifting from the hollows and folds of the hills, and one could just make out dark shadowy figures moving between the rocks and the pine trees. They were still some distance away but as they came closer, it could be made out that this was a heavily armed Pakistani patrol returning from an all-night ambush. They were wearing greatcoats and balaclavas[1] to protect them from the cold. They were armed with rifles, Sten machine guns and the last soldier was carrying a light machine gun. They were moving in single file, very close to the CFL. The nearest post was Badmash and it was obvious that they were returning to it. They were still some distance away, but we could count them. They were ten in number. Having been out the whole night, the patrol appeared to be tired.

Many years earlier, while at the Indian Military Academy, I had learnt about 'shadow patrols'. We were taught that following an enemy patrol through ground held by the adversary was a method to acquire tactical information not available through other means. Here, in front of us, a situation was unfolding, where we could put this concept into practice. I needed information badly about the ground around Badmash, and here was an opportunity presenting itself as a solution for me to obtain the necessary information. If I followed the Pakistani patrol into their area, I would be able to get first-hand information about all possible approaches to the post.

I quickly shared my plan with Naib Subedar Narbahadur Gurung, the forward platoon commander, and Naik Kharkabahadur Gurung, one of his section commanders and they readily agreed to follow me. The enemy patrol had now come quite close and if we were not quick enough, we would miss this excellent opportunity.

I quickly called the CO, but there was no answer and there was not enough time to wait for permission from the CO to go forward. I decided to go anyway. We armed ourselves with khukris, grenades and Sten machine carbines and moved through the safe lane of our own minefield.

Moving quickly and silently, we moved towards the CFL and took position behind a big rock which was on the CFL itself. The enemy patrol had now come very close. We could hear the sound of our own breathing and the steps of the approaching patrol.

A patrol of 4/5 GR (FF) preparing to shadow a Pakistani patrol

The silence was oppressive. The track being taken by the enemy patrol would pass immediately in front of the big rock. The sound of their footsteps grew louder and louder. None amongst the patrol was talking. Perhaps they were too tired and all they could think of was the mug of hot, sweet tea that awaited them at Badmash. If we made the slightest noise, we would be discovered and the odds were in favour of the Pakistanis—ten against three.

However, the Pakistani patrol went past, trudging along wearily. When they had gone some distance, we stealthily followed them in accordance with the practice of shadow patrols, taking care to move in the footsteps of the Pakistani soldiers, so as to avoid enemy booby traps and mines.

As we moved forward, we could now clearly see the ground to the east and west of Badmash and to its rear. We could also see that if we approached the enemy post from the rear, Badmash could be cut off and reinforcements from the Pakistani rear areas would be difficult. This was something important that we were able to learn by coming forward.

The Pakistani patrol moved through their low wire entanglement and the safe lane of their minefield, and went past their sentry post that overlooked the track which they were using. Fortunately for us, there was no sentry at that post at that time.

We could have gone back at this stage, but the opportunity to get more information was too tempting. It was a risk and I took it.

There was a low wall just in front of the langar and we took position behind it, just twenty feet away from the langar.

The whole layout of the post could now be seen. Unfortunately, we had no paper and pencil to make a sketch.

The three of us got down to working out the details of our plan of attack: the approach for the attacking force, the location of the support weapons, the location of the stops, the targets for the mortars and machine guns, etc. The enemy patrol was blissfully unaware of our presence so close to them.

We were so engrossed with our task that we were not aware that a razakar who was cutting grass below the ridge had now reached the track. He now blocked our exit. He had a rifle in one hand and a sickle in the other.

The razakar was astonished to see three Indian soldiers in olive green uniforms right inside their post. He probably thought that there were many more who had concealed themselves in and around the post and that the post was in the process of being attacked. Instead of firing at us with his rifle, he panicked and started shouting, '*Dushman aa gaya, dushman aa gaya! Hamla ho raha hai* (The enemy is here, the enemy is here! We are under attack)' and ran down the slope on which he had just come up.

We were taken by surprise and stood up.

The soldiers of the Pakistani patrol had placed their weapons against the walls of the cookhouse and were enjoying their tea. Listening to this commotion, they stared at us in horrified disbelief. Throwing away their mugs of tea, they reached for their weapons.

We could have fired at the Pakistanis there and then and caused a lot of damage, but that was not the object of our mission. Besides, I did not want to break the ceasefire, so we hurried back through the way we had come.

We had scarcely crossed the enemy minefield and the wire entanglement when the enemy post started firing at us with rifles and machine guns along with cries of *'Allah ho Akbar'*. When we reached the big rock behind which we had sheltered earlier that morning, we came under enemy mortar fire. Luckily for us, the mortar bombs were falling on either side of the track and exploding down below but the machine gun bullets began coming uncomfortably close.

By the time we crossed our own minefield, all our battalion posts were under heavy Pakistani artillery fire. The enemy shells were exploding and throwing up mounds of earth and rocks, and were detonating some of our own mines, making our return more hazardous.

The troops from my post were watching this whole drama quietly and were waiting anxiously for our return. Small fires had broken out due to the shelling and when we emerged through the curtain of dust and smoke, our boys started cheering and clapping.

Meanwhile down below at the base, the CO was having his early morning cup of tea when the noise of the artillery shelling disturbed the tranquillity of a quiet, peaceful day. He quickly picked up the phone and asked the exchange to put him through to all the post commanders.

One by one, in the laid-down sequence, the post commanders were put through to the CO. They all said that their posts were under artillery fire, that there were no casualties till then, that all troops had deployed to face any emergency. When the CO spoke to my post, the CO was told that I had gone into Badmash Post and had not yet returned.

The CO was astonished and perplexed. He could not believe what he was being told. He asked my 2ic what made me go into an enemy post. My 2ic could not answer because I had not briefed him. When I was leaving, I was short of time and all I could do was tell the platoon havildar of the forward post to inform my 2ic that I had gone forward.

At that time, even I had not known that I would go into the enemy post. We had gone forward to see the ground around Badmash and we had entered the enemy post only when we saw there was no sentry at the entrance.

The CO directed my 2ic who had answered his call to tell me to speak to him as soon as I returned.

Further to the rear, the Brigade Commander was out for an early morning walk when the sound of artillery fire reached his ears. He cut short his walk and hurried back to his headquarters. He was met by the Brigade Major (BM), who was the chief operational staff officer of the brigade.

'The Gorkha defences are under heavy shelling, Sir,' said the BM.

'Have you found out why and have you contacted the Gorkhas?' asked the Brigade Commander.

'I have spoken to the Adjutant of the Gorkhas because the CO was busy,' said the BM. 'They have deployed and are ready for action. The neighbouring battalions have also deployed and their reserve companies have been alerted and are moving to their designated locations.'

'What about the guns?'

'They have been deployed, Sir,' said the BM.

'Good,' said the Brigade Commander. 'Find out what has triggered this off. I was listening to this morning's news. Our Prime Minister and the President of Pakistan are in the Soviet Union today at Tashkent negotiating a ceasefire agreement which is being facilitated by the Russian President.'

'We are trying to find out, Sir,' said the BM. 'I have asked all the battalion commanders to investigate what could have been the cause of this firing. The division and corps have been ringing up to find out what happened and why the ceasefire has been broken. I have informed them that we have not opened fire and that the ceasefire has been broken by the Pakistanis and not by us, as this is what all the units had stated. However, the UN observers from the Pakistani side have said that the Pakistanis are alleging that the Indians attacked one of their posts.'

'Attacked them where?' asked the Brigade Commander, who was now quite perplexed. Why was this happening and that too within his brigade?

'Looks like it is in the battalion-defended sector of the Gorkhas, Sir.'

By this time, I had returned and explained the whole situation to the CO.

'Why did you not take my permission before you did something as stupid as this?' he asked.

'Tried to get through to you, Sir, but there was no response, and I could not wait.'

'Are you aware that our Prime Minister is in Russia negotiating a peace agreement with Pakistan? And here you are, starting another war!'

'No, Sir. I did not know. Sorry, sir.'

After a while, the Brigade Commander managed to get through to the CO.

The CO told the Brigade Commander exactly what had happened.

'Has your company commander gone mad? The whole divisional sector has come alive. Questions are pouring in from the division, corps, command and the UN Observer

Group. What do I tell them? Are you aware that the Prime Minister is in Tashkent negotiating a ceasefire agreement with the Pakistanis?'

'Yes, Sir.'

'Where is Cardozo now?'

'He is back, Sir.'

'Have there been any casualties?'

'No, Sir.'

'Anyway, why did he go across in the first place?'

'Well, Sir, he says that he needed information about the approaches to the Pakistani post to make the plan you had ordered him to submit by this weekend.'

'What?' he shouted. 'Is he blaming me?'

'No, Sir. He is not blaming you. He is just saying that he could not get enough information about the approaches to the Pakistani post, so he decided to go across and get it.'

'Has the world gone mad? Send him to me immediately. How much time will it take for him to reach me?'

'About two hours, Sir.'

'Send him to me at once.'

I was in my overalls and had no time to change. I put on a belt and beret and hurried down to the Battalion Base.

The Brigade Commander understood clearly that if the fact that he had ordered me to make a plan for the capture of the post came out, he would have to share part of the blame. The ceasefire was on, the talks at Tashkent were on, the Prime Minister of India was in Russia negotiating the terms for a ceasefire and here not only had an officer from his brigade crossed the CFL, but it could also come out that it was he who ordered the company commander to make his plans for the capture of a Pakistani post—that too at a critical time when the two countries were negotiating a peace agreement. The United Nations observers had joined the cacophony of the division, corps and command asking for an explanation. All that was left was a call from the Army Chief asking him whether his brigade was starting another war!

This was the Brigade Commander's second command tenure of a brigade. What we did not know was that his board for promotion to the Major General rank was due at the end of the year. He had done well in the war and all his good work could now be washed away by this company commander whose energy appeared to exceed his common sense.

When I reached the base, the CO was in conversation with the Brigade Commander. I could overhear only the tail-end of the conversation. The Commander was saying, 'I will have to sort out your officers, if you can't sort them out yourself.' Col. Madan Bhatia was not the type of officer to take nonsense from anyone, of whatever rank. However, he understood the predicament of the Brigade Commander, so he said, 'Cardozo has reached the base, and I am sending him to you, Sir, but please remember that if anyone has to deal with him, it will be me.' With that, he put the telephone down.

I apologized to the CO for what had happened. I also explained that the opportunity that presented itself that morning was too good to be wasted and that there was no time to inform him of what I was going to do. The CO told me, 'No excuses. You have done a stupid thing. However, remember you are a tiger and not a mouse. You will have to take the consequences of your actions like a man. Now go.'

I left for the brigade headquarters in a Jeep that was kept ready for my immediate departure. I rehearsed in my mind what I would say to the Brigade Commander. I had learnt that he was very, very angry.

I later learnt that the CO initiated some damage control to mitigate the enormity of the rashness of my action.

He called up Brigadier Fridell, the Commander Artillery of the Division, an officer with an excellent reputation, and very close to the General Officer Commanding the Division, who was also a gunner. The CO reminded the Brigadier of a conversation they had some time earlier. Brigadier Fridell had told him that I had visited the Division Headquarters during the 1965 war and had requested for artillery support prior to my taking a large convoy to Poonch after it had been cut off for more than ten days. The Commander Artillery had promised me artillery support but that had not happened. I had to break the ambush and had suffered heavy casualties in the process, and he had felt bad about this. He also reminded him of another instance when the Commander Artillery was unable to provide my Company with artillery support, when we were attacking a feature taken over by a strong force of infiltrators. Once again, I suffered heavy casualties due to the lack of artillery support.

Col. Madan Bhatia felt that this was an opportunity for the Commander Artillery to make amends.

In addition to reminding him about the past, he also told him exactly what had happened, including the fact that the Brigade Commander had ordered me to make a plan for the capture of the concerned enemy post. He highlighted the fact that initiatives by young officers should not be stifled. If I was punished, it would send a wrong message to the rank and file of the division.

The Commander Artillery replied, 'Madan, I am aware of the capabilities of your company commanders. Are you, however, aware of what is happening just now at Tashkent?' 'Yes', said the Colonel, 'I have learnt about this only just now.'

'Okay', said the Commander Artillery. 'I'll go to the Brigade Headquarters and see what I can do. The GOC is perturbed about all this as the corps, command and the UN Observer Group are asking questions. I'll take his permission and go.'

In the meanwhile, news about what had occurred spread like wildfire from post to post along the Indian side of the CFL and the reaction at the posts was strange.

It was laughter!

Laughter because it was always the Pakistanis who instigated trouble along the CFL, and it was always we who were held accountable. For the first time, the Pakis were at the receiving end, and they had panicked without even a round being fired! Their reaction only indicated how insecure they were! These reactions had been conveyed to the Brigade Commander by the Brigade Major, but the Commander was not amused.

I arrived at the Brigade Headquarters and met the BM, 'Tiger' Thyagraja. The BM met me with a big smile. He was from the Parachute Regiment and never lost his cool.

He said, 'The commander has asked me to march you in, but I'm not going to do that because we are of the same rank. He is walking up and down in his office like a caged tiger. He is very upset. Are you aware that the Prime Minister is in Tashkent with the Russians and the Pakistanis negotiating a peace agreement?'

With that, he opened the door and let me in.

The Commander was not walking up and down like a caged tiger. He had finished with that, and he was now sitting down at his desk ready to eat me up!

'May I come in, Sir?' I asked.

'You stupid fool. Did you ask the Pakistanis that, when you entered their post?'

'No, Sir.'

'Then why did you go across the Cease-Fire Line and enter an enemy post without anybody's permission? What made you go into an enemy post?' he asked, adding, 'Are you in your senses? Are you aware that by crossing the CFL, you have violated the ceasefire agreement?'

What was the use of telling the Brigade Commander that this was the best way to execute his own orders for the capture of Badmash and that the best way was to follow the Pakistani patrol into their own post, that I had no time to inform anyone, that no harm had been done and that the Pakistanis had over-reacted?

I remained silent.

'I asked you a question and I demand an answer. Answer me.'

'I just wanted more information to make a good plan, Sir.'

'What plan?'

'The plan you asked me to make, Sir.'

The Commander nearly hit the ceiling. He seemed terribly agitated.

'You stupid idiot,' he shouted. 'Did I ask you to cross the CFL? Did I ask you to enter an enemy post?'

'No, Sir.'

'Then why did you do such a stupid thing? Are you aware that the Prime Minister of India and the President of Pakistan are in Tashkent negotiating a peace agreement? And here you are about to start another war! What do I do with idiots like you in my brigade?'

'No, Sir.'

'What do you mean by "No, Sir"?' asked the Brigade Commander.

'No, Sir,' I said, 'I did not know that the Prime Minister was in Russia negotiating a ceasefire agreement.'

'You silly man, you have again not answered my questions. Did I tell you to cross the CFL? Did I tell you to enter a Pakistani post?'

'No, Sir,' I said.

Fortunately, at this stage, the BM knocked at the door and announced that the Commander Artillery had arrived from the Division in connection with this incident. 'Ask him to come in,' said the Brigade Commander and told the BM to pull up a chair for the Commander Artillery and to place it next to him. The Commander Artillery entered the Brigade Commander's office and sat down by his side.

I was standing at attention and the BM was told to wait outside.

The Brigade Commander began to tell the Commander Artillery about what had happened. The Commander Artillery interrupted him and, addressing him by his first name, said that he knew all about what had happened, and that the GOC had asked him to intervene and initiate damage control.

'Can I ask this young man some questions?'

'Go ahead,' said the Brigade Commander. 'Maybe you can make some sense of his story, because I can't.'

Addressing me, the Commander Artillery said, 'I have spoken to your CO and I know the whole story of your adventure across the CFL. Now listen carefully to my questions and answer me truthfully.

'Did you kill or wound any Pakistani soldier?'

'No, Sir.'

'Did you fire any weapon?'

'No, Sir.'

'Did anyone from your picquet fire any weapon to cover your return?'

'No, Sir. No weapon of any sort was fired.'

'Good. Did you leave any evidence of any kind inside the Pakistani post? A scrap of paper? Anything?'

'No, Sir.'

'Good.'

'Have you any idea as to why the Pakistanis have reacted like this?'

'No, Sir.'

Addressing the Brigade Commander, the Commander Artillery said: 'I have spoken to the CO of the Gorkhas, and after getting the whole account from him, I briefed the GOC and gave him the outline of what had actually happened. He has directed me to initiate damage control. He has asked me to check on all matters concerning this incident and to speak to the UN officers across the CFL to prevent this matter from blowing up any further. I have already told the UN Observer Group that the Pakistanis are jittery and have unnecessarily overreacted when one of our patrols lost their way and crossed the CFL and came up to one of their posts. Indiscriminate firing by the Pakistanis has caused unnecessary damage to our posts and it is they who have broken the ceasefire and put the peace talks at Tashkent at risk. The UN Observer Group as well as the Pakistanis are more anxious than us to put a cap on this incident. The corps and command are also keen to close the matter, considering what is happening in Russia. The GOC has asked me to check all facts before proceeding further. Can I speak to the GOC?'

The Brigade Commander seemed to be happy with the way the issue was now progressing and that his part in this incident would not be discovered. He called the signal exchange and asked to be put through to the GOC.

While waiting for the call to come through, Brig. Fridell said, 'Incidentally, the Gorkhas have done very well during the war in a number of actions and the GOC knows about it.'

Just then, the call to the GOC came through.

Addressing me, the Brigade Commander said, 'Get out and stand outside. Tell the BM to also stand by.'

I saluted and got out as quickly as I could. The BM was already standing outside. He put his finger to his lips and motioned me to keep quiet.

Brig. Fridell spoke with the GOC. The conversation was clearly audible from where we were standing. It was not our intention to eavesdrop, but we were only following orders to wait, and frankly we were also keen to know what was being said.

Brig. Fridell told the GOC that he had spoken with the Brigade Commander and with me, and he was satisfied that there was no evidence whatsoever left at the Pakistani post and that neither the Gorkhas nor anybody else had fired a shot in retaliation. He also told the GOC that he had spoken with the UN Observer Group and that they had in turn spoken with the Pakistanis, and that all concerned wanted the incident to be amicably resolved.

The GOC said something that we could not hear but from the conversation it appeared that the GOC wanted to know what should be done with me.

Brig. Fridell said, 'Sir, you would be aware that the Gorkhas had done well during the war and even though this officer has created a situation that could have well been avoided, it shows clearly that we are in total control of the ground up to the CFL and beyond, and that is good. If this young officer is punished, it would send a wrong message to the young officers of the division with regard to initiative, boldness and courage, and that should not happen.'

The GOC said something else that we could not hear and Brig. Fridell responded, 'Yes, Sir. First, we could send him on leave so that he does not talk about what has happened. Secondly, we could issue a Special Order of the Day to say that although courage and initiative are well appreciated, balance and maturity are also needed in the execution of tasks, particularly along the CFL and that it is important to keep seniors informed of action contemplated—something like that—and yes, Sir, I will keep BGS Corps and Command informed.'

The Brigade Commander did not know what to say. He was relieved to hear what the Commander Artillery had said, mainly because his part in the episode would not come out now and even if it did, it showed offensive action on his part, which was not bad. The whole issue had now turned around completely, and both he and I were now being projected in a more positive light.

Basically, he also realized that my action across the CFL was not that bad, after all. It had, in fact, raised the morale of his troops and that was a good start for his command tenure of the brigade. He also realized that he needed to work in closer cooperation with the commanding officers of his brigade and not to have preconceived notions about them, and to trust them more.

However, the issue of how to deal with me remained.

Brig. Fridell came to my rescue once again. He said to the Brigade Commander: 'Did you know that Cardozo had got engaged just before the war and that he is to get married within a few months? And did you know that ten days' casual leave to make the arrangements for his wedding had been cancelled because of your visit to his post? Would it be a good decision if he is sent on ten days' casual leave to cool off?'

The Brigade Commander must have thought it was a good idea because it would put a cap on the fact that he had ordered me to make plans for the capture of an enemy post. He called out to the BM to come inside.

The BM grinned and gave me a 'thumbs up' and went in to the Brigade Commander. He returned and said that I was wanted inside.

I entered and saluted. I knew exactly what had transpired because we had overheard all that was said.

The Brigade Commander cleared his throat and said, 'I have been thinking about this whole issue and considering what the Commander Artillery has said about your going across the CFL and what has happened thereafter, two issues emerge. One, you need to think twice about major decisions that you are sometimes forced to take. And if you have to violate a rule, make sure that you keep your superiors informed. Also, when you break a rule, you must be prepared to accept the consequences.

'Considering that you acted in good faith, I am letting you off this time. You are being sent on ten days' casual leave to think about what you have done and to cool off. Your plan for the capture of Badmash must, however, reach the Brigade Headquarters before you leave and no funny stuff this time. Now, beat it before I change my mind.'

I said, 'Thank you, Sir,' saluted and left. The BM was all smiles. We shook hands and I left for my battalion, my company and my men. I was finally able to go on leave to make arrangements for my wedding which took place in April that year.

So, in retrospect, it is a matter for consideration as to who was the real 'Badmash' in this episode! Was it the

Pakistani post that got jittery and used excessive force against an imagined attack, or was it a young officer who, without permission, crossed the CFL and entered an enemy post to make his plan for a raid, or was it the Brigade Commander who did not want it to come out that he had given the officer an order to make a plan to raid a Pakistani post?

Maybe, a bit of the *'badmashi'* falls on all three!

Postscript

Ultimately, as far as the brigade was concerned, all turned out well. The Brigade Commander was promoted to Major General; I got my leave and the episode of my crossing the CFL and entering an enemy post was given a decent burial.

Unfortunately, at the national level, things did not go well at all! Our brave Prime Minister Lal Bahadur Shastri, who had given orders for the opening of the second front in Punjab, passed away at Tashkent and we had to give Haji Pir back, after capturing it with so much effort and sacrifice.

The manner in which decisions were taken during the period of this incident was excellent. The Army had officers at all levels who responded to issues without having to check all the way up the chain of command to get clearance for local level actions. Risk-taking was part of the decision-making process. As a consequence, leaders at all levels had the confidence to do what they thought was right and were assured of the backing and support of their seniors. This incident strengthened that understanding.

Going across the CFL was not exceptional. They were called raids. Today, they are euphemistically called 'surgical strikes' and receive a lot of press coverage. In those times, thankfully, nothing appeared in the press. The media needs to understand and accept that overexposure of these types of incidents has an adverse impact on the security of future operations.

Sometime later, an incident occurred that gave me, my battalion and the Army much to reflect on.

Tensions had once again risen between India and Pakistan, and the battalion was informed that Pakistani forces would attempt a raid on one of our posts. In addition to extensive patrolling up to the CFL and the laying of ambushes, link patrols cleared areas between our posts. On one particularly pitch-dark night, a link patrol approached an area where the battalion had laid an ambush. The lookout of the ambush party, who was a Lance Naik, challenged the approaching patrol and asked the patrol leader to identify himself. Three times the challenge was given and the patrol leader failed to respond. The lookout fired five rounds and all five bullets found their mark. The leader of the patrol, who was a JCO, was killed and four members of the patrol were wounded—so accurate was the marksmanship of the lookout on that dark night.

The battalion was in a quandary. Was the lookout justified in opening fire? If unjustified, should he be punished?

A Court of Inquiry was held and it cleared the Lance Naik of all blame. In this incident, it was a case of a patrol leader forgetting the password on a dark night with zero visibility and the firer could therefore not be blamed.

Sometimes, strange things happen in the life of the military, and commanders at all levels need to look at such incidents dispassionately with due balance and maturity, keeping in mind the characteristics of the troops involved. Their decisions have far-reaching effects on morale, which is an important principle of war.

12

The 1965 War—Success or Failure?

'No one starts a war—or rather, no one in his senses ought to do so—without first being clear in his mind what he intends to achieve by that war and how he intends to conduct it.'

—Carl Von Clausewitz

There has been much debate about whether the outcome of the Indo–Pak war was success or failure. This has to be looked at by both sides with logic and not jingoistic hyperbole.

If an aggressor decides to launch an offensive against another country and fails to achieve its aim and objectives, then the obvious conclusion should be that its failure is equivalent to a defeat. Similarly, if the country against whom the war was initiated succeeds in defending itself and thwarts the aims of the aggressor, then it should rightly be concluded that it has achieved a victory.

There have been some suggestions that the war was a 'draw'. Even in football, hockey or cricket, there is no such thing as a draw. In football, penalties decide who is the winner and even if that fails to produce a result, then it is 'Sudden Death' that decides the winner and the loser. A similar system exists in hockey. Even in cricket, there is no such thing as a draw. If the teams playing cricket score an equal number of points, then the team with the better run-rate is considered the winner.

Similarly, in war, there is no such thing as a draw—it is either victory or defeat. Even if the result of the war is inconclusive, there are parameters that should decide who has got the better of the other and that should decide who has won the war. In the context of our subcontinent, those parameters are: the amount of enemy territory captured, the destruction of the enemy's war machine and the ability to destroy the opponent's capability and will to fight.

Pakistan failed miserably in its aim of annexing Jammu and Kashmir even though it was a major national aim and all factors were heavily loaded in its favour—politically, economically and militarily. In facing Pakistan's offensive, India decided that the best option was to open a second front and draw the enemy's armour and infantry into the war and destroy Pakistan's offensive forces. In this, India substantially succeeded.

Pakistan lost 1528 sq. km of territory while it held just about 554 sq. km of Indian territory. India was successful in destroying more than half of the armour of Pakistan's 1st Armoured Division in the greatest tank battles fought since World War II at Phillaura, Khem Karan and Sialkot. Pakistan lost 170 tanks in this war against India's losses of twenty-nine tanks destroyed and forty damaged. Of the

Pakistani tank losses, thirty-two were in good running condition! In other words, Pakistan lost most of its armour and it was forced to call off its offensive in Punjab. It also failed in its capacity to continue the war because it had run out of ammunition. In the context of these parameters, it is clear that India had won the war. India should never have agreed to the ceasefire and should have continued to go for a fight to the finish. Unfortunately, the same mistake has happened in all the wars that we have fought with Pakistan: 1947–48, 1965, 1971 and 1999. Every time, we have given in to a UN call for a ceasefire and each time, we have let Pakistan off the hook, allowing her to recuperate and carry out her next misadventure.

Afterword

'If you must play, decide three things at the start: the rules of the game, the stakes and the quitting time.'

—Chinese Proverb

The 1965 Indo–Pak war was a complex all-out war fought on a much bigger scale than the Indo–Pak wars of 1947–48, 1971 and 1999. It extended from Ladakh in the north, to Bikaner in Rajasthan in the north-west and across the states of J & K, Punjab, Rajasthan and West Bengal. At that time, there was no Northern Command, nor was there a 16 Corps. What was then being handled by one Western Command is being handled today by three commands. The war started as a localized conflict in the state of J & K and exploded into an all-out war across the boundaries of the states. As always, our intelligence failed us, although there were enough indicators to understand what Pakistan was up to.

It must also be remembered that I Corps, 6 Mountain Division and other units and formations that took part in this war were raised just before the war and had no time nor opportunity to train or get their act together. My own unit, the 4th Battalion the 5th Gorkha Rifles (FF), was raised on 1 January 1963, and we were holding the CFL in Jammu and Kashmir within six months of being raised. The battalion, at that time, did not have all its authorized equipment nor had we the time to carry out collective training. Being a newly raised unit, it was composed mostly of recruits. It was only on 1 August 1965 that the battalion was allowed to come down from the CFL for collective training. However, the enemy struck with Operation Gibraltar on 5 August and that collective training never happened. Instead, the men had to learn from hands-on experience in actual war how to fight as sub-units and units. This was the situation at that time and considering the outcome, I think we did pretty well.

This book attempts to bring to the reader what happened in the Indo–Pak war of 1965, through a collection of stories that describes some important battles and the experiences of individuals who were part of those battles. However, it needs to be remembered that history often repeats itself and what happened before, during and after a war casts a shadow on the future. At present, the future points in the direction of another conflict that looms menacingly on the horizon. This time it is most likely that there will be collusion between Pakistan and China against us. India is a rising power, and no one, particularly China and Pakistan, want to see India do well. The US and Europe look at India with a jaundiced eye. Although the US considers China as a rival and India as a bulwark against China, to rely on the US, in my opinion, would be a big mistake. Pakistan continues to be the US's favourite protégé and an analysis of past conduct, including its conduct in the Indo–Pak wars of 1965 and 1971 and the war in Ukraine, is a warning to us to be wary.

In such a war, it will not be difficult to forecast the groupings of the protagonists. It will be safe to assume that the US will support Pakistan. It had sent part of its Pacific fleet to the Bay of Bengal in the Indo–Pak war of 1971 to intimidate us and had led the West against us in the corridors and conference halls of the United Nations. Britain also sent a pack of destroyers into the Arabian Sea to create a pincer movement in collusion with elements of the American Pacific Fleet to intimidate India. Russia, at that time, came to our rescue both in the Indian Ocean and in the UN. However, it is difficult to predict what Russia will do now, in the backdrop of the Ukraine war. Although the Russians are grateful for India's political support, China has gone out of her way to support Russia politically, economically and with material resources. It is likely, therefore, that when push comes to shove, Russia will be part of a China–Russian alliance. At best, it will be neutral as far as we are concerned.

Therefore, we must hope for the best and plan for the worst. It is on the cards that we shall be alone in this two-front war and we need to gear ourselves for that eventuality. This includes not only a faster move to be self-sufficient in weapons and equipment but also to ensure that the jawans are well trained, and that the Army morale is not eroded by ill-conceived policies like 'Agnipath'. Time is at a premium!

When looking back at the 1965 war, which is the subject of this book, we need to consider what happened in that war and the wars that followed and take stock of our strengths and weaknesses. Errors committed in the past should not be brushed under the carpet from a false sense of loyalty. I have, through these stories of courage, tried to bring out the pluses and minuses of our plans and conduct that shaped that war. Courage among leaders at the unit level was of a high order. It is the decision-making at higher levels of military planning that was found wanting and is deserving of more attention.

Although we did not do too badly, we could have without doubt done much better. There is no satisfaction in declaring that 'It was a draw'! In war, there is no such thing as a 'draw'. The only outcome that we should look forward to is victory.

Issues that need to be taken note of because of the 1965 war are given below:

Greater Jointsmanship among the Services

Cooperation between the Army and the Air Force was found to be wanting. The ground forces were bereft of air support whereas the PAF was very much in support of the Pakistan Army. Instead of accepting this shortfall, the IAF has consistently been on the defensive to say that interdiction was their priority. In a future war, this cannot be allowed to happen. There needs to be a balanced approach to interdiction and support of ground troops with judicious allocation to both needs. Cooperation between the three services is a must, and this includes the Indian Navy. Cooperation is a principle of war and this must be developed to a high standard of excellence.

Theatre-ization

Whereas the reorganization of the armed forces from the concept of 'commands' into theatres has been accepted, the progress, for whatever reason, has been excruciatingly slow. If the government has also accepted that this is how the armed forces need to be reorganized, then there needs to be some degree of urgency in this matter.

Synergy between the Armed Forces and the Government

The success achieved in the 1971 war clearly established the existence of a high level of synergy between the government and the service chiefs. This synergy evaporated on the conclusion of the war. In an unprecedented decision, the armed forces were excluded from the Shimla Conference—something that has never happened in any war worldwide! The results are there for all to see. What was won on the battlefield was lost on the conference table. This synergy needs to be restored during both peace and war.

Vision, Strategy and Planning

From the manner in which all the wars have been fought on the subcontinent, it appears that India only reacts to moves by our enemies. We seem to have developed a defensive mindset perhaps because the national policy appears to prefer a peaceful outlook and approach. Be that as it may, it needs to be understood that although India does not believe in acquiring what is not ours, it needs to accept that 'offence is the best form of defence'. Also, the nation needs to have a clear vision as to where we want to be at least ten years down the line—politically, economically, militarily and socially, so that all the ministries, the three services and the paramilitary services can work out their own visions, infrastructures, missions, aims, objectives, policies, procedures and activities.

At the conclusion of each war, a review needs to be taken to assess the pluses and minuses of the conduct of the war. The Indo–Pak war of 1965 is no exception.

Glossary

Army Terminology

AA: Anti-aircraft

FUP: Forming up place—a place where troops form up for the assault, square to the objective that has to be captured.

SL: Start Line—forward line of the FUP.

H-Hour: The time set for an attack to commence.

Section: A body of ten infantry soldiers armed with small arms, part of a platoon.

Platoon: Three sections make a platoon. It is headed by a JCO.

Company: Three platoons make a company. It is commanded by an officer, normally a major. It has a headquarters with basic facilities of a communication system and supporting arm detachments attached to it.

Battalion: An infantry unit consisting of four rifle companies, a support company with supporting arms and an administration company to provide logistics support. It can operate independently with certain added elements.

Brigade: Can be an infantry, armoured or artillery brigade. It is headed by a brigadier. An infantry brigade normally has three battalions. It has a headquarters with supporting staff and communication systems. Normally, it is part of an infantry division but can also be independent.

Division: Can be an infantry or armoured division. An infantry division normally has three infantry brigades with a whole range of supporting arms and logistics units. It can operate independently.

Corps: It normally has three infantry divisions with additional formations added to it depending on its allotted task.

Strike Corps: A formation with an offensive task. Normally grouped with an armoured element, it could be an armoured division or an armoured brigade.

LMG: Light machine gun.

MMG: Medium machine gun.

Troop: A generic term for a body of soldiers. Specifically, an armoured troop consists of three tanks. An artillery troop consists of three guns and forms part of a battery.

Battery: An artillery sub-unit consisting of three troops.

Squadron: An armoured formation consisting of four troops and a headquarters.

Patrol: A body of infantry soldiers tasked to recce ground to access information regarding enemy defences or to get some specific information. It could be of the strength of a section, platoon and sometimes a company when required to fight to get the required information.

No man's land: Ground between opposing forces not held by either side.

RCL: Recoilless anti-tank gun.

RL: Rocket launcher.

Adjutant: Staff officer who assists a commander in his duties. He normally deals with discipline, parades and ceremonial matters.

Quartermaster: Staff officer who assists a commander with regard to logistics and administration.

Brigade Major: Staff officer at a brigade headquarters who deals with operational matters.

DQ: Short for DAQMG, i.e., Deputy Assistant Quartermaster General—staff officer at a brigade headquarters who deals with discipline, logistics and administration.

Subedar: Senior junior commissioned officer.

Havildar: Equivalent of sergeant. A senior non-commissioned officer.

CQMH: Company Quartermaster Havildar.

CHM: Company Havildar Major.

Air Force Terminology

Bogey: Enemy aircraft.

Pigeons back to base: Part of a dialogue between the pilot and radar controller where the pilot is asking for directions and distance back to base.

Racecourse pattern of attack: A pattern of attack when a target is repeatedly attacked by the same aircraft and no air or serious ground opposition is expected.

Wingman: Pilot who flies aircraft in support of the leader.

Scissor manoeuvre: Criss-cross aerial combat manoeuvre between two aircraft where each pilot tries to get his aircraft into a position of advantage over the other.

Buster: Use of maximum available power of the aircraft.

Mush into the ground: Aircraft descending into the ground due to inertia.

Dogfight: Aerial combat between two or more aircraft.

Break port: Sudden hard turn to the left.

Pitot tube: Slim tube in front of an aircraft or mounted on the wing to measure air pressure.

Long finals: When an aircraft makes a long approach while coming in to land.

Notes

Synopsis

1. Arjun Subramanian, *India's Wars 1947–1971* (Noida, Uttar Pradesh: HarperCollins, 2016).
2. General K.V.K. Rao, PVSM, *Prepare or Perish* (Lancer Publishers Pvt. Ltd), p. 119, para 2.
3. Haji Pir Ops. For more details, see *Behind the Scene* by Major General Jogindar Singh, VSM (New Delhi: Lancer International, 1993), p. 110.
4. Op Gibraltar: Ibid., pp. 106–11.
5. Lt Gen. V.K. Singh, PVSM, *The Indian Army: A Brief History* (New Delhi: United Service Institution of India, 2007), p. 110.
6. Shiv Kunal Verma, *1965: A Western Sunrise* (New Delhi: Aleph Book Company, 2021), p. 62.
7. Ibid., p. 62.
8. Rear Admiral Satyendra Singh, *Blueprint to Bluewater: Indian Navy 1951–1965*, p. 420.
9. General K.V.K. Rao, *Prepare or Perish*, p. 123, paras 4 and 5.
10. Major General Jogindar Singh, VSM, *Behind the Scene*, p. 98.

11. Lt Gen. V.K. Singh, PVSM, *The Indian Army: A Brief History*, p. 114.
12. Strike Corps: An army's strategic reserve. Used for offensive/counter-offensive operations in accordance with previously conceived plans. Consists normally of an infantry division grouped with an armoured division/brigade.
13. *The First Round: Memoirs of Air Marshal Asghar Khan of Pakistan.*
14. *Transition to Triumph: The Story of the Indian Navy 1965 to 1971*, p. 35.
15. Ibid., p. 30.
16. Ibid., p. 35.
17. Vice Admiral Mihir K. Roy, *War in the Indian Ocean*, p. 86.
18. Ian Cardozo, *Beyond Fear* (Gurugram: Penguin Random House, 2023).
19. Lieutenant General V.K. Singh, *The Indian Army: A Brief History*, Chapter 5, 'Winds of War'.

Chapter 1: Combat above Kharagpur

1. Shiv Kunal Verma, *1965: A Western Sunrise*, p. 252, para 2 and p. 255, para 2.
2. Ack-ack: The nickname given to anti-aircraft guns.
3. Bogies: Enemy fighter aircraft.
4. Pigeons back to base: Parts of a dialogue between a pilot and a radar controller where a pilot is asking for directions and distance back to base.
5. Racecourse pattern of attack: A pattern of attack when a target is repeatedly attacked by the same aircraft as no serious air or ground opposition is expected.

6 P.V.S. Jagmohan and Samir Chopra, *The India–Pakistan Air War of 1965*, p. 184, para 3.
7 Break port: Sudden hard turn to the left.
8 Pitot tube: Slim tube in front of an aircraft or mounted on the wing to measure air pressure.
9 Long finals: When an aircraft makes a long approach when coming in to land.

Chapter 2: At the Gates of Lahore

1 Rifle Company: A sub-unit of an infantry battalion, which consists of about a hundred men.
2 From conversations with the author.
3 Brigadier Desmond Hayde, MVC, *The Battle of Dograi*, USI Pamphlet, New Delhi, 2009, p. 11, para 2.
4 No-man's-land: Ground between own forces and the enemy.
5 Jitter: To create fear and panic in an opposing force.
6 Verey lights: These were flares used for signalling and lighting at night; they came in several colours and were fired from a pistol.
7 DF tasks: Defensive Fire tasks—preselected target areas that are likely to be used by an enemy attacking force on which artillery fire can be called for.
8 Brigadier Desmond Hayde, MVC, *The Battle of Dograi*, p. 11, para 2.
9 Ibid., p. 19, para 2.
10 Ibid., p. 23, para 2 and p. 24, para 1.
11 TDU: Tank Destroyer Unit.
12 T-16 Carrier: A small tracked vehicle meant to carry an infantry battalion's mortar detachment.

Chapter 3: Valour Personified

1. Company Quartermaster Havildar (CQMH): A senior non-commissioned officer in charge of administration of a rifle company.
2. RCL: Anti-tank recoilless guns.
3. Zeroing of a gun involves all actions taken to ensure the proper alignment of a weapon so that its round hits the target.

Chapter 4: Asal Uttar

1. Shiv Kunal Verma, *1965: A Western Sunrise: India's War with Pakistan* (New Delhi: Aleph, 2021), p. 239, para 3.
2. My own assessment. However, corroborated by Air Marshal Subramaniam in his book *India's Wars: 1947 to 1971*, HarperCollins, p. 269, para 2.
3. ORBAT: This gives out the names of the formations and units that would take part in a particular battle along with its supporting arms and administrative units.
4. Shiv Kunal Verma, *1965: A Western Sunrise*, p. 245, para 3.
5. Ibid., p. 244, para 2.
6. Capt. Amarinder Singh and Lt Gen. T.S. Shergill, *The Monsoon War: 1965 India–Pakistan War* (New Delhi: Roli Books, 2015), p. 214, para 7 and p. 215, para 1.
7. Notes from Amarinder Singh and Lieutenant General T.S. Shergill, PVSM, *The Monsoon War,* p. 214.
8. Ibid. p. 214, para 3.
9. Ibid. p. 214, para 4.

Chapter 5: Chhamb Battleground

1. This title is a derivative of the title of the book *Battleground Chhamb* by Maj. Gen. A.J.S. Sandhu, VSM (New Delhi: Manohar Publishers and the United Service Institution of India, 2017).
2. 'O' Group: A group of military officers who take orders for a military operation from a superior commander.
3. Shiv Kunal Verma, *1965: A Western Sunrise: India's War with Pakistan* (New Delhi: Aleph Book Company, 2021), p. 151, para 4.
4. Ibid., p. 150, para 1 and p. 151, para 3.
5. Ibid., p. 148, paras 1 and 2 and p. 150, para 3.
6. Ibid., p. 150, para 1.
7. Ibid., p. 151, para 1.
8. Ibid., p. 154, para 4.
9. Maj. Gen. A.J.S. Sandhu, *Battleground Chhamb*, pp. 61–62.
10. Shiv Kunal Verma, *1965: A Western Sunrise: India's War with Pakistan*, p. 150, para 2.
11. Maj. Gen. A.J.S. Sandhu, *Battleground Chhamb*, p. 61.
12. Shiv Kunal Verma, *1965: A Western Sunrise: India's War with Pakistan*, p. 153, para 2.
13. Ibid., p. 155.
14. Maj. Gen. A.J.S. Sandhu, *Battleground Chhamb*, p. 65.
15. Maj. Gen. A.J.S. Sandhu, *Battleground Chhamb*, p. 62, para 4.
16. Shiv Kunal Verma, *1965: A Western Sunrise: India's War with Pakistan*, p. 156. paras 1 and 2.
17. Ibid., pp. 156–58.
18. Ibid., pp. 160–61.
19. Ibid., p. 155, para 1.

Chapter 6: The Avengers

1. Shiv Kunal Verma, *1965: A Western Sunrise: India's War with Pakistan*, p. 148, para 2; p. 151, para 1 and p. 157, para 2.
2. P.V.S. Jagan Mohan and Samir Chopra, *The India–Pakistan Air War of 1965* (New Delhi: Manohar Publications, 2009), p. 70, para 2.
3. Shiv Kunal Verma, *1965: A Western Sunrise: India's War with Pakistan*, p. 74, para 2 and p. 161, para 1.
4. P.V.S. Jagan Mohan and Samir Chopra, *The India–Pakistan Air War of 1965*, p. 77, para 3.
5. Ibid., p. 79, para 2.

Chapter 7: A Mission Fulfilled

1. P.V.S. Jagan Mohan and Samir Chopra, *The India–Pakistan Air War of 1965* (New Delhi: Manohar Publications, 2009), p. 139, para 3.
2. Air Marshal Bharat Kumar, *The Duels of the Himalayan Eagle*, pp. 140, 142.
3. To find out what happened to Tubby Devayya, please read his story 'It's Never Too Late' in *Beyond Fear* by Ian Cardozo (Gurugram: Penguin Random House, 2023).
4. P.V.S. Jagan Mohan and Samir Chopra, *The Indo–Pak Air War of 1965*, p. 140, paras 1 and 3; Shiv Kunal Verma, *1965: A Western Sunrise: India's War with Pakistan*, p. 263, para 2.

Chapter 8: Ambushed!

1   *The India-Pakistan War of 1965*, Ministry of Defence, Government of India, p. 284, para 3 and p. 55, para 1.

Chapter 10: Twists of Fate

1   The bridge and the enclave were given to Pakistan according to the Agreement of 1959, which similarly gave control to India of the bridge at Sulaimanki in the Hussainiwala Sector.
2   Troop: This consists of three tanks and an armoured squadron has four troops.
3   Identity discs: At that time, when the Indian and Pakistani armies went to war, each soldier carried two discs on a chain around his neck that gave his name, his army number and his religion. This ensured his identity and in the event of being killed in battle, the manner in which his body would be disposed of according to the religious rites of the individual. One disc was interred with his body and the other kept for purposes of record.
4   General K.V.K. Rao, *Prepare or Perish* (Delhi: Lancer International, 1991), p. 211, paras 2, 3 and 4.
5   Ibid., p. 211, para 4.
6   Ground of Tactical Importance (GTI): The most important ground critical for the defence of a battalion-defended area/brigade-defended sector.
7   'The Last Post': A bugle call that signals the end of fighting. It is also a tribute to those killed in battle.

8 'The Rouse': A bugle call that gives hope that those who die in war are lifted to live again in the memory of their country and that they have gone to their god.
9 'Shush': My own word to describe the effect of the breeze on the trees that overshadowed this scene.

Chapter 11: Badmash

1 Balaclava: Also known as a monkey cap, balaclava helmet or ski mask, it is a form of cloth headgear designed to expose only part of the face, usually the eyes and mouth.

Bibliography

'Study the past, if you would define the future.'

—Carl Von Clausewitz

Brigadier A.A.K. Chaudhry (Pakistan Army), *September 65: Before and After* (Dehradun: Natraj Publishers, 1991).

Amarinder Singh and Lieutenant General T.S. Shergill, *The Monsoon War: 1965 India–Pakistan War* (New Delhi: Lustre Press, Roli Books, 2015).

Air Vice Marshal Arjun Subramaniam, *India's Wars: A Military History: 1947–1971* (Noida, Uttar Pradesh: HarperCollins Publishers India, 2016).

Air Marshal Bharat Kumar, PVSM, AVSM, *The Duels of the Himalayan Eagle* (Gurgaon: IMR Media Pvt. Ltd, 2015).

Charles Chenevix Trench, *The Indian Army* (Thames and Hudson, 1988).

Brigadier Desmond Hayde, MVC, The Battle of Dograi, USI Pamphlet, New Delhi, 2009.

George MacMunn, *The Martial Races of India* (Delhi: Mittal Publications, 1979).

Lieutenant General Harbakhsh Singh, VrC, *War Despatches: Indo–Pak Conflict, 1965* (New Delhi: Lancer International, 1991).

Major General Jogindar Singh. *Behind the Scene: An Analysis of India's Military Operations 1947–1971* (New Delhi: Lancer International, 1993).

General K.V. Krishna Rao, PVSM, *Prepare or Perish* (New Delhi: Lancer Publishers Pvt. Ltd, 1991).

Maj. Gen. Lachman Singh, PVSM, VrC, *Missed Opportunities: Indo–Pak War 1965* (Dehradun: Nataraj Publishers, 2005).

Manvendra Singh (ed.), *The Indo–Pak War 1965*, Defence and Security Alert, Volume 6, Issue 11, New Delhi, August 2015.

General Mohammad Musa, H.J., *My Version: India–Pakistan War 1965* (New Delhi: ABC Publishing House, 1983).

Sir Olaf Caroe, *The Pathans* (Karachi: Oxford University Press, 1996).

S.N. Prasad and U.P. Thapliyal, *The India–Pakistan War of 1965: A History* (Dehradun and New Delhi: Natraj Publishers, on behalf of the Ministry of Defence, Government of India, 2011).

Shiv Kunal Verma, *1965: A Western Sunrise: India's War with Pakistan* (New Delhi: Aleph Book Company, 2021).

United Service Institution of India, 'The Battle of Dograi', pamphlet issued by the USI, Kashmir House, Rajaji Marg, New Delhi, as part of a series of important battles.

Lieutenant General V.K. Singh, 'Winds of War—The 1962 & 1965 Conflicts', *The Indian Army, A Brief History*, Chapter 5, (New Delhi: Centre for Armed Forces Historical Research, United Service of India, 2005).

Scan QR code to access the
Penguin Random House India website